THE ONE I'LL ALWAYS REMEMBER

Caring for America's Wounded Warriors

GARY L. BLOOMFIELD

LYONS PRESS

Guilford, Connecticut

An imprint of The Rowman & Littlefield Publishing Group, Inc.
4501 Forbes Blvd., Ste. 200
Lanham, MD 20706
www.rowman.com

Distributed by NATIONAL BOOK NETWORK

British Library Cataloguing in Publication Information available

Library of Congress Cataloging-in-Publication Data available

ISBN 978-1-4930-3861-9 (cloth : alk. paper)
ISBN 978-1-4930-3862-6 (electronic)

♾™ The paper used in this publication meets the minimum requirements of American National Standard for Information Sciences—Permanence of Paper for Printed Library Materials, ANSI/NISO Z39.48-1992.

CONTENTS

CONTENTS

CONCURRENT MISSIONS

HOME FRONT

FOREWORD

Have you ever wondered how the medical personnel who care for our nation's "wounded warriors" feel? What goes through their minds? How do their encounters with these brave wounded combatants affect them, sometimes for the rest of their lives? How do they cope with the visual realities of caring for those who defend us and are willing to sacrifice everything doing it?

The One I'll Always Remember is an emotional and compelling compilation of real-life, sometimes surreal, recollections of medical personnel who have provided care to America's wounded warriors during military campaigns in Iraq and Afghanistan, plus a handful of stories from other hot zones, such as Somalia, Berlin, and Liberia. Some of the most poignant stories are from the home front.

This book includes the remembrances of medical personnel writing about "The One" patient who has had a dramatic impact on them, consequently revealing the human side of those caregivers, and the array of emotions they experience. One of the physician assistants who contributed to this book wrote about an Iraqi girl injured by a suicide bomber at a family wedding. A night nurse recalled prepping the body of a deceased soldier, talking with him through the night. These are just two of the many stories recounted in *The One*.

US Army photojournalist, video-cameraman, newspaper editor, and veteran Gary Bloomfield is an award-winning, widely published author and editor of multiple books and magazine articles, not to mention photographic coverage of worldwide military events. He has served for more than ten years in the Army and another fourteen as an Army public affairs chief, documenting the conflicts, successes, and casualties of war. Of note is his book *Duty, Honor, Victory: America's Athletes in World War II* (Lyons Press), which won the Benjamin Franklin Award. While serving on the Korean DMZ in 1976, Gary was named Army Journalist of the Year. These are only a few of his accolades in military photojournalism. Bloomfield continues to pursue and validate accurate, real-life documentation of

America's wars, her sacrificial warfighters, and her military caregivers . . . giving credit where credit is due.

Being asked to write the foreword of Gary Bloomfield's latest book was not only an honor for me, it was a *requirement* he demanded for the validity of the project. Gary wanted a medical care provider who had been *personally* involved in caring for our country's military men and women to write the foreword. "I want this book to pay tribute to both our military and nonmilitary medical personnel and the wounded warriors they care for," he said. "Those who have cared for our nation's wounded warriors or other victims of our conflicts, whether it's on the battlefield, at a field hospital, on a medevac flight, on a warship, or stateside in a military hospital or a VA facility. The book has more credibility by relying on those who are in the thick of it on a daily basis, who know better than anyone else the efforts they go to every day to do what they do."

I felt I could not contribute to the documented memories recorded in this book. I had a difficult time trying to isolate "The One" out of the many veterans I have cared for in my life as a nurse. To me, they *all* were memorable. Consequently, Gary Bloomfield asked me to consider writing the foreword.

Having served in a US Air Force security police squadron during the early 1970s Vietnam conflict, I have some military experience. I have been a registered nurse for over twenty-five years, during which time I provided multifaceted, specialized care for America's servicemen and women in areas such as pre-hospital treatment and transport, emergency departments, critical care and burn units, interventional radiology, surgery, and post-anesthesia care units. It has been and continues to be a privilege, and debt, for me to deliver the finest medical care to our nation's wounded warriors, who are numbered among the most honorable, dedicated heroes one could ever expect to meet.

Medically and surgically "salvaging" my military brothers and sisters has been an emotional rollercoaster. After a duty shift, I have wept bitter tears in those moments alone, knowing there will be more dedicated young men and women who literally will "give their all" . . . *their* freedom . . . to keep America, her children, and her allies free from tyranny. Compounding these heart-wrenching events, we also think of the heroes at home—the spouse who has to take up the slack due to their mate's absence, the concerned mate daily dreading that possible "notification visit" from their spouse's commander . . . that "line of duty death."

We have further shared the same thoughts in the break-rooms . . . that these mostly *young* brave men and women have willingly sacrificed what most Americans take for granted . . . a life to be *lived*, with hopes and dreams and plans for the future. Most of our warfighters considered the price of freedom to be worth the cost of death or dismemberment, in order that their country and their families could be safe to have a future, and enjoy the things other Americans enjoy. Their bravery and sacrifice is one of the primary driving forces behind the high-quality, professional, competent care we medical personnel strive to deliver.

In reading these accounts it is vital to understand the basic working environment of military medical personnel. Stateside and foreign-soil fixed-base medical operations care usually occur in one specific treatment area such as an operating suite or a medical-surgical unit. Then the patient is transferred to another area, where a different provider takes over.

In combat theaters, such as Iraq or Afghanistan, medical care can be most commonly referred to as "continuative," meaning once the combat medic delivers the wounded warrior to the forward-operating base field hospital, the medic may, based upon the mission situation and their provider level-of-care, continue providing life-sustaining care for their patient by following their patient from the trauma/operating room to the post-anesthesia area, then to the holding area.

It may be necessary to just surgically stabilize the warfighter and air-evac him or her to the nearest fixed-base hospital, which leads us to the next phase, the treatment arena in the air. In aeromedical evacuations caregivers must follow different principles of treatment depending on air-pressure gradients (whether the aircraft is pressurized or not). These conditions can instigate a more significant stress-load on both the caregiver and patient, especially during an extended flight that might take hours.

The One I'll Always Remember puts you on the front lines and in the operating room as you read and experience these stories alongside the military care providers. You will feel the emotional and psychological trauma of extended combat surgeries, and learn about coping skills, such as avoiding knowing a patient's name or too much personal information. More than 95 percent of all the wounded warriors who come to the field hospitals leave the facilities alive, yet it's those few who don't make it who haunt medical personnel for years, sometimes forever. They bear the guilt of not being able to save everyone, asking if possibly they could have done more. They may not know their patients' names, but they see their faces in haunting memories, even decades later.

—Larry Mahana, RN

INTRODUCTION

They come in broken, battered, muddied, bloodied, and burned; their accoutrements of combat are shredded, shattered, splintered, and often embedded in gaping wounds. Any damaged tools needed to wage war can simply be replaced . . . but a mortally wounded combatant cannot.

The cynics of war think otherwise. A soldier dies, but there are a thousand new recruits trained every month to take their place. A Marine pays the ultimate sacrifice—"Semper Fi" . . . next!

In addition to bombs and bullets, the logistics pipeline from stateside supply depot to the front lines includes fresh bodies to fill the ranks depleted by America's continuing war on terrorism. Those fresh bodies are often pimple-faced teenagers, still too young to vote or too young to drink, and much too young to die. Some might consider death the best option, knowing the alternative might be debilitating life-changing injuries. In fact, many wounded warriors wonder why God spared them, when death would have been so much easier.

But for the doctors and nurses, physician assistants, combat medics, and many more health care providers charged with tending to our nation's wounded warriors, they know every casualty is someone's son or daughter, a mother or father, a brother or sister, a friend, neighbor, or coworker. They are charged with providing the best medical care possible, even against impossible odds. But after years of trauma surgery, they may become hardened to what seems like an endless stream of broken bodies; but they're not heartless.

They care, maybe a little too much. Maybe the job would be a little easier if they didn't care so much. For every hundred lives they've saved, there's another one they couldn't . . . and that's the one they can't forget. For some, they never forget that one. For all the countless hours, the chaotic rush of incoming casualties, the assembly line of carnage, followed by the sheer boredom waiting for the next rush, there's sometimes an unexpected miracle that makes it all worthwhile. There's always that special one who beats the odds stacked against them.

Casualties of war come in battered and broken, muddied and bloodied, many of them anxious to get patched up so they can get back into the fight, others considered "incompatible with life"—via helicopters, transport planes, armored vehicles, or carried in on stretchers. AIR FORCE PHOTO

I wondered, were there health care providers in the aid stations, field hospitals, trauma wards, emergency rooms, rehab clinics, and burn centers who actually gave a damn about the wounded warriors they treated and cared for?

Was the nasty side of war really nothing more than meatball surgery, operating on nameless warfighters who had the misfortune of surviving an IED blast, a mortar attack, a convoy ambush, or a sniper's bullet? During their training, were they ever taught the true meaning of compassion, and did they know how to convey that with honesty? Or did military expediency push aside any emotional attachment they might have for their patients? Did they shove their emotions in a dark corner no one else could see, yet in reality find it impossible to ever let go of the memories of the battered, bloodied, and broken?

During a year-long tour at an aid station or field hospital in a war zone, they might see hundreds of battle-related casualties. Over the course of a lifetime in trauma medicine, they'll see thousands more and, unfortunately, they can't save them all. But was there one among the many—just one of our nation's wounded warriors—who had a personal impact on each of these dedicated caregivers?

Maybe it was a young soldier who came in more dead than alive and was given Last Rites, clinging to life. But somehow God reached down and decided this one should stick around a little longer.

Or maybe it was a Marine with what appeared to be a superficial flesh wound, demanding to be patched up so he could rejoin his buddies still engaged in a firefight. But then a few hours later he's dead, and everyone wonders, what the hell did they miss?

Or maybe it's a child, caught in the crossfire, an innocent victim of war's brutality. Some doctors and nurses deployed to a war zone have admitted those are the hardest to deal with, the children who remind them of their own little ones back home.

In their own words, our military's health care providers tell about the one combatant they can never forget. Some are miracles who shouldn't be among the living. Some are amputees who refuse to be called disabled, or paraplegics and quadriplegics who accept their fate with grace and dignity, who would do it again if it meant saving some other American from going to war. And yes, despite their best efforts, some of those they remember didn't make it, buried with full military honors, in gardens of stone.

But they remember those bloodied and battered combatants who they may have only cared for during moments of chaos in the emergency room, or whom they sat with through a quiet night in the ICU, waiting for the end to come. Or they counted the reps in rebuilding muscles that had atrophied, or stood close by, ready to catch an amputee learning how to walk again. Or they endured verbal assaults while changing the dressings of a burn victim. They remember them all.

They may not recall the names, but they can't forget Sergeant Rock from Dallas, who joked that he could somehow figure out a way to fire his weapon without any arms, or Don Juan from the Bronx, a quadriplegic who wanted his motorized wheelchair rigged with a turbo charger. And whatever happened to Surfin' Byrd, who said he'd be up on his board and shooting the curl again at Oahu's North Shore in two years? On one good

Another fallen American hero, given a farewell with full military honors, buried in a garden of stone. ARMY PHOTO

leg! If anyone could do it, he'd be the one. And, oh my God, what about Psycho Charlie? Mainlined Red Bull every time his patrol went outside the wire. Or that female Humvee driver—everyone called her Roxie—talk about cussing a blue streak! Everyone avoided her in the mornings until her coffee kicked in, black with five sugar cubes.

And that baby-faced chaplain's assistant, who swore he was legal age to drink even if he looked thirteen. The bartender thought he had a forged ID the first time he hobbled into the club. They figured he was just an Army brat, still in high school. Wrong place, wrong time when he got hit by a sniper's bullet. Or remember sweet old Master Sergeant Duke—everyone called him Marmaduke because he looked so hangdog? Just one day walked off the hospital grounds and hasn't been seen or heard from since.

Seems like everyone had a nickname, not always flattering but it's how they were remembered. Even the doctors and nurses had their own monikers, some only whispered behind their backs—like Nurse Ratched and Doctor Clueless, or that notorious surgical team of Tweedledee and Tweedledum, the latter better known as Dumb Dumb among his peers: well deserved, by the way.

Every hospital has a nurse known as Hot Lips and that other pair of studs known as Dr. McDreamy and Dr. McSteamy, though the old-timers usually don't know who anyone's referring to. There's usually a Bones or two, a Dr. Demento and a Dr. Frankenfurter roaming the halls. And the entire M*A*S*H crew is usually well represented, from Hawkeye and Trapper John on down the line to Radar and Klinger and Hot Lips.

There were plenty of pompous surgeons vying for the role of Charles Winchester, and a few inept ones who played Frank Burns to a T. And even in today's politically correct, racially sensitive world, one or two Spearchuckers might show up every now and then.

And, just as in the fictitious 4077th M*A*S*H, typically it takes an entire team of caregivers to rebuild a wounded warrior's body and give them a decent quality of life. Despite the comic overtones though, trauma medicine is serious business, often with deadly consequences. The health care providers may not suffer any physical pain or lose anyone close to

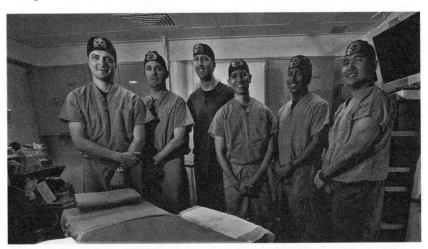

Every military hospital staff has its Hawkeye and Trapper John, Dr. McDreamy and Dr. McSteamy, Hot Lips and Nurse Ratched, even Radar and Klinger, plus a few inappropriate nicknames (surgical team on board the carrier *Carl Vinson*).
NAVY PHOTO

them in combat, but in this extended war on terrorism, fought over multiple battle fronts, there is an emotional toll, and often they suffer it in silence. Burnout is one of the lingering effects of many years treating our nation's wounded warriors. They may be smiling even while fighting back the tears, but often deep inside they're hurting, often for years, without anyone even knowing it, and they certainly don't forget. It's impossible to forget.

Some say writing a book is like slicing open a vein and letting the emotions bleed all over the page. *The One I'll Always Remember* gives our nation's medical professionals an opportunity to tear down some walls they've built, share their experiences of a time they can't forget, and remember that special One . . . a wounded warrior, maybe an innocent bystander, a helpless child who was brought to them broken and bloodied, and who touched their heart like none before or since.

—Gary L. Bloomfield

IRAQ

For the American soldiers and Marines serving in that maddening fishbowl known as Iraq, it's a matter of deciding who looks most like they have evil on their mind.

After their brutal dictator Saddam Hussein was deposed and the celebrating subsided, everyone expected miracles. Overnight Baghdad would be transformed into the crown jewel of the Middle East once again. Saddam's stashed billions would pay for it all. Or so they all thought.

After the Shock and Awe bombing campaign, constant roadside ambushes, and years of self-inflicted sectarian violence, what they've been left with is a city more closely resembling Armageddon. They're living the end of days, struggling just for clean water and a few hours of electricity.

The entire country is a hotbed of hostility, aimed at the foreign occupiers, including humanitarian aid workers from western countries.

In a country where weapons are more plentiful than diplomacy, anyone with a grudge can take out their frustrations on the American infidels they see every day, patrolling their neighborhood, convoying down the roads, manning the checkpoints.

That uncertainty is what American men and women have had to deal with every day since hostilities began almost thirty years ago. Suspicious of everyone, trusting no one, except those Americans standing beside them and guarding their six. And for good measure, some have found religion (even if only temporarily), and have carried little trinkets—good luck charms—to keep them safe.

But sometimes the soldiers' vigilance just hasn't been enough, and that's why combat medics and Navy corpsmen have accompanied nearly every foot patrol and convoy that has ventured into the viper's den. It's why medevac helicopter crews have been on standby 24-7, ready to take off in minutes and land in dangerous hot zones, to pick up the wounded and get them to forward-based aid stations and field hospitals, knowing how vital the golden hour is in saving lives.

❦

Improvements in body armor have resulted in more combatants surviving devastating injuries. But at the same time, the number of amputees has risen dramatically, since the appendages aren't as well protected. "Dr. Chuck" recalls one such patient who barely survived the street fighting in Fallujah, Iraq.

Getting Stung in the Hornet's Nest

My first deployment was to Afghanistan fairly soon after 9/11, and for classified reasons we actually didn't get called too much. I was a fresh major. We had nine missions over six months, enough to get our feet wet, know we had a tight team, and feel pretty comfortable with our mission. Sure our guys were getting shot, some burned, but nothing much worse than a party weekend in Detroit.

Our second deployment found us in Iraq, just as the hornet's nest known as Fallujah was getting cleaned up and the Sadr City push was just beginning. Our first mission was five days after our arrival in Iraq. We were sent to move a soldier who had been standing on an improvised explosive device when it exploded. That he was even alive was incredible, of course.

As was the case for so many of our soldiers, the depleted-uranium-reinforced Kevlar body suit saved his torso. As the blast originated from below, the twenty-one-year-old male's head was relatively uninjured. Both his arms and legs, however, didn't fare so well—they were gone. It wouldn't be the last time I saw patients mangled to this extreme, but this was my first one.

You'd be amazed how easy it is to keep just a torso alive. Without arms or legs, there's no "meat" for the blood to pump through. Exceptionally healthy heart and lungs are not challenged to provide oxygen to just a head and body. Pain is minimal, compared to burns and fractures (no arms and legs means no fractures). There isn't much for us to fix, just clean and dress the stumps—"all bleeding stops, eventually"—put tubes in lungs, bladder, and stomach, set up the ventilator and add a bit of morphine, and you're off. Within a few hours of his encounter with the IED, we were ready for the six- to seven-hour flight from Iraq to Germany, where he would receive more extensive surgery at Landstuhl Hospital.

American patrols in Iraq and Afghanistan were vulnerable to improvised explosive devices. Body armor protected their torsos but not their extremities. Advances in trauma care have improved survival rates, but some, with multiple amputations, brain injuries, and severe burns and blindness, wonder if they'd be better off if they hadn't survived. ARMY PHOTO

The flight to Germany seemed uneventful to my team and our patients. Our other patients had various abdominal or chest injuries that required our presence just in case, but their injuries would mend nicely. Frankly, we had little to do except ensure the ventilators were working and our patients were comfortable.

Not so for the rest of the plane. Flights on the C-17 often had one hundred patients or more, but typically only four to six of those required critical care. The walking wounded sit in chairs along the fuselage, facing inward. There are no curtains or walls—just a brightly lit tube about twenty-four feet in height and diameter.

Everything and everyone is open to observation in the cargo hold. Thus, the remaining space was taken by soldiers with minor injuries (just severe enough to require care in the rear and possibly a return to home stateside). In addition there might be civilians on board who needed specialist visits, and cargo that needed to get to the United States. Often these minor cases were more than eager to regale pretty nurses with stories of how they earned their war wounds and—given the intensity of combat at that time—any reason to fly out of Iraq to safety in Germany made for good morale.

But on this flight, the mood turned suddenly somber as we arrived with our "torpedo" piled high with bleeping monitors, ventilator, suction machines, and IV pumps. No one could miss the fact that one litter was only half full compared to the others. For six hours, these passengers watched us tend to our multiple-amputee patient. Word got around that we hoped to get this twenty-one-year old soldier home to his newly-wed wife and six-month-old daughter. We all wondered what their future would hold. I watched a full-bird colonel break down in silent tears, away from the others on board.

Fast forward to 2012. I'm a colonel-select myself now, six deployments come and gone, and I'm assigned to one of our major military facilities

When a combatant is wounded on the field, it's imperative to get them medical care as quickly as possible. Medevac helicopters often mean the difference between life and death. ARMY PHOTO

where we receive those very patients from overseas to complete their care. I enjoy 7:00 a.m. to 4:00 p.m. hours teaching young captains and majors to do what I do while tending to the patients in the intensive care units (ICUs).

This spring-like morning, I'm walking to the hospital from my car, when I notice a young soldier sporting a flat-top and riding in a motorized wheelchair ahead of me, presumably for a doctor's appointment. I have no idea why he caught my eye—such sights are common here. Perhaps it was the fact that he was missing both legs. Perhaps, as I overtook him, it was my surprise to see he had two prosthetic arms with which he drove the wheelchair.

Or maybe I unconsciously registered the "jar-head" was shaped a lot like the guy I flew with in 2003. Nope . . . none of that was what made me stop and observe him. What caught my attention was the adorable, blonde-haired, blue-eyed seven-year-old girl, gleefully hugging her daddy and planting kisses on his cheek while he let her ride on his lap. They were laughing together, but I could not hear them.

It was my turn to have silent tears.

—"Dr. Chuck"

War is a messy affair and often, when there's collateral damage, innocent civilians get added to the body count. During the war in Iraq, thousands of civilians were killed or injured, mostly by sectarian violence, but the American presence there along with other Coalition forces, was a constant, encouraging foreign fighters to converge on Iraq to take on the mighty western "infidels." Air Force Capt. Scott Brocious, serving as a nurse at the Field Hospital in Balad, Iraq, can't forget a little girl injured in an explosion.

Princess in Pink

Only a few hours earlier, she was just a little ragamuffin, playing with cousins and other family members who had journeyed to Baghdad for this special occasion, a wedding. I imagined that those who hadn't seen her in a while would remark how big she'd grown, what a young lady she was becoming. She wasn't used to sitting still while her mother painted her toes and fingernails a pastel pink, and combed her hair, slowly turning her precious daughter into a little princess, with a frilly dress and a satiny pink ribbon to match her nails. The final touch was white shoes she'd rarely worn before, due to all the dusty roads and flatland outside.

She was just four years old, but for days she could feel the excitement of this festive occasion building, and now it was finally wedding day. All of the women in the village were involved with making it a special day for the bride. And it should have been a day of joy and pride, but instead it quickly turned to tragedy, when two unknown women dressed in robes approached the crowd and unleashed their hatred, detonating concealed explosives.

The carnage was devastating and deadly. We don't know all of the details, probably never will. But we can't forget the little princess who came into our field hospital, battered and burned, just one among the many. The call had alerted us just minutes earlier, "MASCAL, local civilians," and we waited for any number of injuries. The military term mass casualty doesn't tell us much more than to brace for hell. Soon after, they arrived. She was just one of the ten, her face and appendages peppered with fragments from the blast.

Many of the others were much worse off, but one of the other nurses looked at her tiny body and cried out, "She still has nail polish on." We all

"The carnage was devastating and deadly . . . we can't forget
the little princess who came into our field hospital battered and
burned . . . peppered with fragments from the blast." ARMY PHOTO

couldn't help but look. Pink. We checked the other casualties and asked
relatives about her mother, who thank goodness was not one of those we
were treating.

As nurses we try to keep our emotions in check, which makes it easier
to handle the brutality of war, the constant barrage of trauma in a war
zone. We typically refer to our patients as numbers or by their injuries,
such as "the guy with the amputation in bed 4," or simply "surfer dude."
Names are too personal. This intentional distance, a subconscious for-
getfulness, gives us some protection from the brutality humans inflict on
others. But when innocent civilians are caught in the line of fire, especially the children, it's impossible not to think of our own loved ones back
home.

That's why something as commonplace as pink nail polish sucker
punched us and forced us to face the reality of the moment. We thought

of her mom meticulously applying the polish to her tiny nails, a mother-daughter moment we had experienced with our own little ones. And of course we wondered if we would ever make it back home to give them a long overdue hug and spend quiet moments together again.

She was someone else's princess, but we all provided a little extra TLC while she was with us. Weeks later an uncle came in and told us her mother had spotted the two strange women approaching, heard them shout their evil intent, then quickly shielded her daughter from the blast as best she could. Sadly, a little princess, an innocent Iraqi girl caught up in the ugliness of war, will never again spend a quiet moment with her mom. All she has is pink nail polish to remind her how much she was loved. And for those of us who were there, pink nail polish will always mean more than it probably should.

—Air Force Capt. Scott Brocious, Registered Nurse

"Never give up. Never give in. Never *ever* quit": This is a motto many military combatants believe in. It drives them forward on the battle-field, when every instinct may tell them to pull back, lick their wounds, and fight another day. It is especially important to motivate our nation's wounded warriors, who often struggle to find reasons to carry on. They may never be whole again, but they will make the most of what remains of their broken bodies.

Learning to Run

I walked onto the ward, my shoes squeaking on the newly buffed floor, my scrubs starched and pressed and my hands shaking a bit from what I was about to do. I'm not real sure but it's also quite possible my knees were knocking, because after all, it was my first day as a newly trained poly-trauma nurse, and I was about to meet the first Marine I would be assigned. He had been injured during the brutal fighting in Fallujah, Iraq.

As I was standing just to the side of the entrance to his room, about to knock on his door, my thoughts went back to how my journey to this point had started. It was February 2001 and I was at a cabin north of Hibbing, Minnesota, surrounded by friends, and as we sat at the breakfast table the last morning of the weekend someone said to everyone: "Hey are you doing now what you dreamed of as a kid?" The question went around the table until it was my turn.

I sat there for a long moment, thinking, "It never occurred to me to ask this question of myself or answer it." I looked up from my plate of pancakes and admitted, "I always dreamed of being a nurse and specifically an Army nurse."

Months went by and that weekend slipped into a distant memory; however the words I had spoken kept swirling back until one afternoon I decided to do something about it. I contacted a nursing school, the first one that advertised "weekend college for working adults," and filled out the admission form. I had not, at this point, truly entertained the idea. I filled out the form assuming I might get a no and then I could remove the thought from ever popping up again and carry on. I received a form letter in the mail explaining there was a waiting list and it might be a year or two until they would have an opening.

Ready to put the idea of becoming a nurse behind me, I did not give it another thought until months later when my phone rang and I was advised there was an unexpected opening and I had been admitted for the fall semester.

I am a believer in God and I pray, and throughout this whole process I had prayed and believed that if this was the path I was supposed to take then a way would be made where there seemed to be none. My first day of nursing school was Tuesday, September 11, 2001.

Knocking on the door of the Marine's room, I heard him before I laid eyes on him, and the tone and pitch of his voice reminded me of the sound of a kid who had just been through something unimaginable and was in need of reassurance and protection. I had a vague thought of the challenges that lay ahead.

As I entered the room, I saw a young man full of bandages and tubes, and most notably there was a large bandage wrapped around his head. My nose picked up a strange sickly smell I could not identify. I introduced myself and he looked right through me, a look I would later become very familiar with. He acknowledged me with indifference and so began my first day.

As I have had the opportunity to reflect back on that first day and what followed, it's a wonder I made it through the first week. I had such high expectations of myself as a nurse, of the others on the nursing staff, and of this Marine. It is a good thing I did not know any different. I had every expectation that he would fully recover, be able to lead a life that, while different from what he might have planned, would still be reward-ing and valuable. So that is how I approached my care planning for him. I would be tough on him, and he was definitely going to be tough on me and every other nurse who would provide care for him throughout his year-and-a-half-long course of recovery.

My dream of being an Army nurse did not pan out; however my desire to care for wounded servicemen and women did. In August of 2005 I was encouraged to attend a job fair the Minneapolis VA was having. My mother had heard about it and thought it would be a great opportunity for me. I argued with her that nothing ever came out of job fairs. In all my wisdom and knowledge, I flatly refused to go, justifying to myself that

An IED exploded as his vehicle was driving past it. A chunk of metal and the debris sliced through his helmet. MARINE CORPS PHOTO

it would be a big waste of time. Still, a small voice nudged me and before I knew it my car was heading south toward the VA in downtown Minneapolis. I arrived at two o'clock and by three I had been given a conditional offer of employment to start the next month, September 2005, as one of the first poly-trauma registered nurses to be hired outside of the VA system.

The first three months of this Marine's recovery were tough. At just twenty-one years old he had witnessed his best friend dying during his first tour in Iraq, made it unscathed through his second tour, and was injured by an IED hidden in a Dumpster on his third deployment.

It detonated while his vehicle was driving past it. He had massive injuries to his brain. The IED delivered more than just the blast: A chunk of the Dumpster and whatever filth had been in the Dumpster prior to the blast had sliced through his helmet, effectively taking off a part of his skull and his brain. His head wound was contaminated and required wound cleaning and debriding daily. He also had a traumatic brain injury that impaired his ability to control his emotions, actions, and outbursts, he had short-term memory issues, and the blast had also left him paralyzed on one side. He was prone to fits of anger and acting out on this anger.

Many people talked about him as already being over with, and I heard things like "Well, if he ever makes it out of here he will either be in jail or dead soon after he is discharged." His behaviors were extreme and this Marine had injured members of the staff by throwing items, breaking things off the wall, and busting a sink off its moorings. But I refused to give up on him: not because I had not questioned in my own mind all of the things others were saying about him but because he was a representative of the freedoms I enjoyed every day. He volunteered, he effectively went in my place, and he took that blast for me and every other American. But while others only saw a damaged Marine, what I witnessed on a daily basis was a Marine who refused to give up.

There are many stories about heroics on the battlefield but very few about the battles and fortitude of the wounded during their recovery. I have been given the greatest honor and that is to "care for him who has borne the burden," and entrusted with a precious vocation to use my skills, knowledge, and abilities as a nurse to bring healing and to protect life, and also to be an advocate and to fight for those under my care.

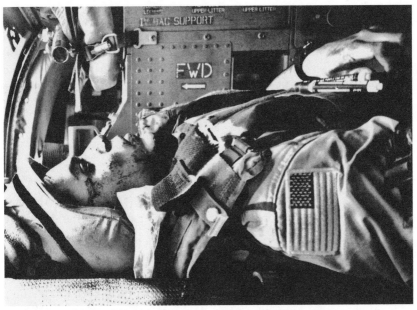

". . . others only saw a damaged Marine . . . I witnessed on a daily basis a Marine . . . who refused to give up." Though in constant pain, he endured hell to get his life back to some semblance of normalcy. AIR FORCE PHOTO

This Marine was in constant pain every day; it was difficult for him to relearn how to walk, how to eat, how to put his socks on, how to shower, and all the things we take for granted on a daily basis. I saw beads of sweat on his brow as he struggled to stand on his own for the first time post-injury, but not once in that year and a half did this Marine ever give up. Not once. Ever. He fought through the pain, the frustration, the anger, the setbacks, and waking up every day realizing he was lying wounded in a bed at the VA and his life would never be the same.

In some ways his journey and mine were connected, intertwined. His path was not one of his choice, but a path he had agreed to when he raised his hand and took his oath as a Marine. My path was one of my choosing and one that began years before when I dreamed about being an Army nurse, but didn't become reality until I was called up.

I believe in a life led in response to being called. Everything up to that point in my recent past had led me to be a nurse for this particular Marine. My service in the Army Reserves and National Guard prepared me to understand the military culture, to be able to have something in common with him—not that I would fully understand or know his specific journey, for that belongs to him alone. But it did provide me with the skills necessary to make a connection with this Marine, resulting in a therapeutic relationship that would help promote all the work being done by the various therapists, the doctors, and everyone involved in his care. This Marine had survived against all the odds; his medic had to convince a trauma team to work on him as his injuries were so catastrophic he was not expected to live.

At the same time, I was learning to stand on my own two feet as a nurse, going through the fire, making mistakes and adjusting to the new environment I had been placed in. This Marine was too. The difference being I was there for him; I was one nurse along the path who was willing to be utilized so this Marine could heal and be successful in whatever he would choose to do. He had been chosen to live.

If I had not been a believer in God prior to working with this Marine, I definitely would have been after. Too many things came together in his story for there to be any other explanation than that he was being called for some unknown purpose, post-injury. My proudest moment as

It might take him a little longer than anyone else, but writing a book about his experiences gives this Marine purpose . . . a mission, a reason to get out of bed . . . a reason to keep on living. MARINE CORPS PHOTO

a poly-trauma nurse, up to that point, was observing this Marine on his discharge day, after being told for months he would be lucky just to walk again, let alone ever run out the front door of the VA. But in fact, he was walking, talking, running, and he was able to make decisions for himself. The last I had heard, he was working at a part-time job and was writing a book about his injuries, his struggles, and his accomplishments. Semper Fi Marine!

—Connie Bengston, BSN, RN, PHN

A sniper's bullet has a nasty sting. If it travels straight and true, it can enter the human body small and exit much larger. But if it hits bone along the way, it can ricochet through the body, ripping into vital organs, hitting bone again, meandering at high velocity with devastating effectiveness. As an Army ICU nurse in Iraq, Maj. Virginia Vardon-Smith witnessed all too often the damage done by snipers' bullets.

A Father Shows His Appreciation

During the summer of 2006 I worked at Ibn Sina Hospital in Iraq, deployed there with the 10th Combat Support Hospital out of Fort Carson, Colorado. I was a critical care nurse working in the ICU in the hospital located in the Green Zone in Baghdad. We were very busy with incoming casualties due to the heavy action taking place in Sadr City. This particular morning, we had been given a report that a seriously wounded soldier was coming in with a significant vascular injury to his left shoulder area.

Our role, with any of our seriously injured soldiers coming in, is to do emergency surgery, and stabilize them for their quick transition out of Iraq and on their way to the American hospital in Landstuhl, Germany. As the charge nurse that morning, I was assigned to this patient. I did my normal checks for things needed at the bedside, filled out paperwork, and checked out our new cellphone soldiers could use to touch base with their families once they were awake and alert enough to talk. Our phone wasn't working so I called down to the Patient Administration section and asked to borrow their phone. I remember this very clearly as I had to argue with a major and actually had to put her in At Ease! As unpleasant as it was, my patient would be coming out of surgery within a half-hour, I didn't have time to argue, and I needed a phone that worked! And I needed it now. I later had to apologize, but that was after my patient had been flown out.

I received an update from Anesthesia at the bedside that a high-caliber round literally tore all the major vessels in his left shoulder (the brachial plexus) and he had had a very significant vascular repair including his aorta. He was lucky his medic on the scene told him, "Don't let anyone take this dressing out of this wound or you will die!" He followed

The injured soldier was in the turret of his Humvee when he was hit in the shoulder and the bullet entered the gap in his body armor, devastating the major vessels, including his aorta. Quick thinking by the medic on site saved his life.
NAVY PHOTO

the medic's instructions to the point where he argued with the Emergency Department doctors when they were trying to evaluate his wounds when he arrived.

The soldier was in the turret of a Humvee when he thought they had hit a bump in the road and he lurched backwards. In fact, he had been shot. As he squatted down inside the hatch, his vest opened just enough for him to spray the inside of the vehicle with blood, splattering the driver who immediately alerted the medic on the radio. The shot entered just at the crease of his body armor at his left shoulder, and when he had his arms across his chest holding his weapon, he had inadvertently applied pressure to the wound. But when he squatted down, he relieved the pressure and the aorta was open, like a burst water pipe!

So, after the anesthetist finished his report, this young specialist began to wake up. He was a bit groggy at first but soon came around. Though he was battered and bruised and bandaged up, I couldn't help but notice his reddish hair and freckles, a typical cornfed beau. I told him about his surgery and that he was safe and should be heading to Landstuhl soon, and he asked if I could call someone back home for him. He gave me his parent" number and I dialed it for him. I waited for it to connect, then ring, and his dad answered the phone. I identified myself, and told him where I was and said, "I have someone here who wants to talk to you" and handed the phone to his son.

They talked and the wounded soldier reassured his dad he was okay and his arm was "fixed" without really comprehending the seriousness of it all. He was certainly glad to be alive, but then he fought back tears and handed me the phone back and said, "He wants to talk to you." I spoke with his dad briefly and answered his questions about his injury and the surgery. I could tell it was all a shock because he measured his questions carefully, and there were long pauses each time I answered him. He appreciated my honest assessment, then we hung up and the specialist had by then composed himself and asked a few more questions about his surgery and requested something for the pain.

We prepared him for transport and within a couple hours, we had him packaged up and ready to head to Germany. I said my goodbyes and reassured him he was going to do well and not to fret but to get better and tell his story to his new and up-and-coming crew.

Well, the story doesn't end there. It only gets better. Fast forward to the fall of 2007. I had returned to Walter Reed Army Medical Center and went right back in the surgical intensive care unit I had worked in prior to deploying to Iraq, and I had recognized the early symptoms of burning out.

I had been caring for blast injury and critical casualties since 2004 when the war had started, from Landstuhl Hospital in Germany, where the critically wounded from Eastern Europe to the Middle East were evacuated; then I attended the intensive care course at Walter Reed in Washington, DC, and remained there to work in the surgical ICU. After six years caring for blown up, blasted, burned, and mangled soldiers, sailors, airmen, Marines, and civilians (including innocent children and enemy combatants), I needed a bit of a break. I asked my chain of command if I could do a little something different for a short while. Not long, just enough to recharge, most importantly so I wouldn't burn out. Of course, this was the time Walter Reed was under the microscope with the wounded warriors and the barracks issues, with the national press corps scurrying around trying to dig up dirt after some family members complained of the living conditions in the barracks. There was some justification for their complaints, and the attention did result in upgrades and improvements. But at this time, when I desperately needed to unwind, no one was going anywhere. However, I was hand selected to be a case manager and one of the original crew to stand up a new unit, the Warrior Transition Brigade.

It was a new concept, to change the focus back to the rehabilitation of the wounded warriors, and I was responsible for thirty-two of our nation's heroes and the management of their outpatient care. One of my soldiers was not at Walter Reed but was located in a civilian facility at the Boston Spaulding Rehabilitation Center, and his father insisted that his son was going to get the best care available, including specialized rehabilitation. So, as a good case manager, I needed to lay eyes on this soldier.

I had been corresponding weekly with my soldier's rehabilitation case manager, the hospital director, and the doctors involved with planning his care. I also worked very closely with the family. So in my weekly phone calls and emails, someone came up with the idea that I should go up and see my soldier and I agreed. I needed to lay eyes on him and ensure they were being totally honest with me, so I could accurately determine the best course of action and discuss his rehabilitation plan with his care team. The wheels started turning on getting me up to Boston, and this facility was so very excited that I was coming. They made all the arrangements including flights, hotels, and meals. So, when I presented this plan to my chain of command, they were thrilled and quickly approved my travel request.

This all happened the first week of December of 2007: On Saturday, December 1, I got married. On Sunday, December 2, I packed my bag and on December 3 I was in Boston. Soon after I arrived, I took a taxi to Boston Spaulding Hospital. It was a very nice facility, and I was greeted by the hospital administrator and her staff. She took me up to the unit where my soldier was accommodated. My soldier's father was a very prominent man with lots of connections, and when I finally caught up with my soldier and his family, they were in the day room where he was participating in a sports presentation during which he was allowed to

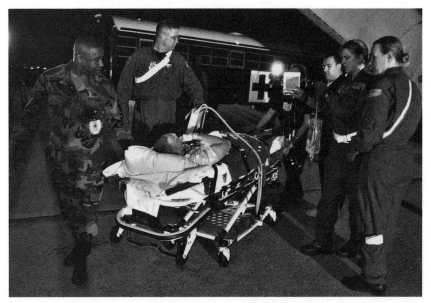

"Our role, with any of our seriously injured soldiers coming in, is to do emergency surgery, and stabilize them for their quick transition out of Iraq and on their way to the American hospital in Landstuhl, Germany." AIR FORCE PHOTO

wear one of the rings the Boston Red Sox had recently earned as World Series champs and got to hold the trophy the team had received. After things settled down and we went back to his room, I finally had time to really assess my patient and his family.

The hospital administrator had arranged a full board review for me about this soldier, including his physical therapist, occupational therapist, speech therapist, neuro-intensivist, dietitian, and pharmacist. There were about fifteen people in attendance to discuss all aspects of care for my patient. After that was done, the hospital administrator asked me if I would mind doing an impromptu presentation to the staff members about how to best facilitate military patients and their families, as this facility was anticipating more military patients in the future. Of course I said yes, and as I entered this room, I was amazed at how many people were there. It was standing room only with approximately sixty people jammed in like sardines. I was a bit taken aback but soon pulled some thoughts together and just began speaking. I sensed they had little experience dealing with military casualties, such as blast injury patients—something I saw way too much of. Nor were they knowledgeable about integrating the military family members as part of the rehab team. We have learned that they are a vital player in the wounded warrior's healing process.

Halfway through, I told the story of the young specialist with the severe shoulder injury, of course leaving out his name, and as I finished, a hand was raised in the back of the room. It was an older gentleman who I thought had a question. As he spoke and stepped forward, I knew exactly who he was . . . he was the father I'd spoken to the day his son was injured during my deployment to Iraq. He said, "You are the angel who said my son was alive and I would recognize your voice anywhere!"

You could have heard a pin drop in the room. I was teary eyed, he fought back the tears, and I don't think there were too many dry eyes in the room after that. As he made his way forward, I met him with a huge hug and we both just cried and comforted each other. (I was personally gratified to know his son, my former patient, had returned to duty, despite some physical restrictions that required continuing rehabilitation. Dad

Once he was stabilized, the patient was prepped for transport, eventually ending up at the Army's Landstuhl Hospital, adjacent to Ramstein Air Base in Germany.
NAVY PHOTO

joked that his son has a hard head and often pushes himself to the limits, so he wasn't at all surprised.) Of course I realized I was still in front of all these people and had to finish my presentation, so I tied it all together, saying we live in a small world and we are all tied together, and through caring and compassion we can come together and help each other along the road to recovery.

At the time of my deployment in Iraq, I was a young Army captain working in a variety of positions: day shift team leader, charge nurse, and staff nurse working with critically ill patients. I had a total of eighteen staff members and one hell of a great head nurse named Maj. Christian Swift. From that deployment, I and three other of my closest nursing friends found the loves of our lives and all of us are happily married, and some have started beautiful families. I am still in touch with my extended Army family members, and we don't go very long without talking or visiting each other. Our takeaway from our experiences in Iraq is that life is just too damned short to waste it on petty BS. We live our lives to the fullest and try damned hard not to have any regrets or any "shoulda, woulda, couldas" in our lives. If we want to go and see or do something, we plan it and do it, because we just never know what tomorrow holds, so we live today as if it were our last.

—Army Maj. Virginia Vardon-Smith, ICU Nurse

In the eyes of a little child, already terrified of the bright lights and strange smells of a US Army hospital, and so many people in pastel-colored pajamas—to them scrubs look like PJs—coming and going at all hours and odd machines sounding like burps and beeps . . . it can all seem very scary. But imagine what a hospital must seem like to a child who's never been to one before, especially one with so many Americans and others there speaking an unfamiliar language. And despite everyone smiling—some maybe smiling a little too much—there's always one of them lurking around with that deadly weapon, what looks like eighteen inches of instant pain, to be avoided at all costs . . . the hypodermic needle.

God Bless the Little Children

In 2006 I was working in the step-down unit as a critical care nurse in Ibn Sina Hospital in Baghdad's Green Zone. The step-down is a four-bed unit for casualties who were originally in the ICU for serious injuries and are now stable enough to leave there but not quite stable enough for the ward.

In the step-down unit, there are two staff members—one RN and one LPN. This particular day it was myself, a captain, and one very high-speed NCO I came to rely on as a valued member of the ICU. She and I worked together like a well-oiled machine. On this day, she and I had four patients: three adults and one child.

The child's name was Awuas (pronounced OW-us), and he was approximately three years old. With sandy brown hair, hazel eyes, and a very light complexion, he was absolutely adorable. He had been left on the doorstep of the hospital with some significant scald burns; we had noticed this kind of injury before coming from some of the local villages around our area. We remembered treating four other children with the same burn patterns, so when we asked the interpreters why they all were burned the same way, they described a horrific scene of what these villages called simply "discipline." In these villages, as the interpreters had described it, they disciplined their children by holding their wrists and ankles and dipping them into hot oil or water. The burn patterns were across their upper back and shoulders, across their upper to mid chests, on their abdomen, groin, and thighs, and up the backs of their calves with no burns to the hands, feet, or faces.

This poor little boy was so frightened of us and in so much pain; it was all we could do to comfort him. The interpreters and housekeepers helped translate, explaining to him how we were going to change his

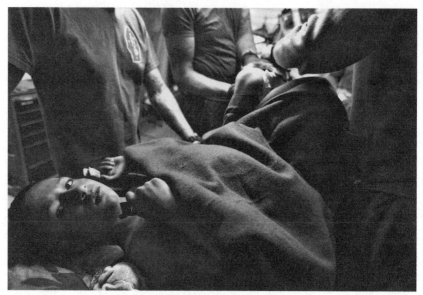

"The child's name was Awuas . . . absolutely adorable. Left on the doorstep of the hospital with some significant scald burns; we had noticed this kind of injury before." His burns were consistent with being held by the wrists and ankles and dunked into scalding hot oil or water, as a form of discipline. He was understandably afraid of strangers, including the medical personnel causing him so much pain while tending to his burns. MARINE CORPS PHOTO

dressings, and give him his antibiotics and pain medicines, but when they wore off, he would wake up, frightened and alone, obviously in pain, and be completely frantic. Some of us had learned enough Iraqi Arabic to be able to talk to him, and it did help most of the time, but sometimes we just couldn't understand him and he couldn't explain what he wanted.

On this day, it was around lunchtime so it was just me, with our three adult patients and little Awuas. It wasn't long before he woke up from a nap and was again in a panic, crying and pulling out all of his IVs, ripping off his oxygen; he was just inconsolable. In previous cases when we had children in the ICU, to soothe them most of the nurses would wrap them in a waterproof bed pad and hold them and sing and rock them on the edge of the bed like we did our own children. This worked most of the time, but often our backs were thrown completely out when we finally got the children to sleep.

We needed a remedy, so I went online and researched portable, collapsible rocking chairs and found them at a sports store. I ordered two because each of our two ICUs usually had at least one child. So, when little Awuas woke up and was pulling everything out, I needed to calm him down quickly. Compounding this problem though were his burns. I had to be very gentle just touching him, but I wrapped him in nonstick bed pads and pulled him into my lap in this rocking chair and began to rock him and sing to him in an attempt to calm him down.

Awuas was not too much younger than my own son, but at that moment he was no longer just an Iraqi child with severe burns who needed some TLC. When you are in that mode you are again back home with your own children, and in that split second, I was rocking my own son, who was badly burned and crying. You can imagine how that tugged at my heart. I did my best to not go there, but the floodgate was open and I just couldn't hold back. I was almost sobbing by the time I got Awuas calmed and quiet. I put him in bed and he went back to sleep, thankfully. I chalked that up to a really bad dream and now he was over it and sleeping peacefully.

I composed myself and went back to work—there's always something to do—and I finished my notes on Awuas and moved on to my other patients. After I checked on everyone, I went back to Awuas's chart and realized he needed an IV antibiotic but had pulled out his IV. That means I had to be the bad guy and stick him, again, to reinsert an IV.

As an experienced ICU nurse, I am pretty

He needed his pain meds and antibiotics but was terrified of the hypodermic needle—absolutely terrified. He screamed and squirmed, making a traumatic experience even worse. AIR FORCE PHOTO

damned good with IVs, but kids are a totally different beast. They squirm and they scream bloody murder, sometimes when they see the needle, and definitely when you stick them, no matter how well you try to explain it to them. So, I gathered up all my equipment—small IV catheter, alcohol, tape, saline flush, extension tubing, clear dressing, and the antibiotics, then I called for an interpreter and hoped they could wake him and begin talking to him, and while he was distracted, I could get things prepped and laid out and get the IV in quickly and hope he wasn't aware of what I was doing until I finished. Nope, this little guy was very switched on and aware of everything going on! As the interpreter walked in, I explained what I needed for him to do for me and how. He said he understood and we began. As Awuas began to open his eyes, the interpreter was talking to him about the uncle he kept asking for, and I started to prep his little arm looking for a good site for the IV. The alcohol was cold, but the interpreter was still chatting away and I found what looked like a good site. I put on the tourniquet and I winked at the interpreter, and he got out his cellphone like he was calling someone and I went for it.

Well, as soon as I made my move, even though I had a pretty good grip on his little arm, he squirmed and jerked and I had to start fishing for the vein, which can be very painful for anyone on the receiving end of an IV catheter. Awuasi let out this wail of pain I had never heard before and started crying and getting hysterical, and he called out for someone, and it was just killing me because he thought I was trying to kill him. I kept fishing for that vein and thought I had it, but he was moving and jerking around too much and when I flushed the line, it infiltrated the saline under the skin and he wailed even more.

I was a complete mess at this point and didn't know why I had become unglued. Exasperated, I abandoned my attempts at starting the IV and called one of my fellow staffers to help me out. When I called out to her and explained what I needed, she asked someone to cover her patient in the unit. When she arrived, I had everything set up. She looked at me and could immediately tell I was "having issues" and asked if I was okay.

"Yes!" I said, even though I was an emotional wreck, because we still needed to get this little boy his much-needed antibiotics. So, we talked about what we were going to do. She was going to stick him while I held him.

I actually contemplated sitting on him and pinning him down, but then I remembered his burns. She prepped his arm again, and he already knew what was coming. The interpreter was reasoning with him that this was for his pain medications and it would make his burns get better, but at this point there was no reasoning with him. As the interpreter was talking to Awuas, he felt the sting of the needle.

The wail that came from this little boy was the saddest most painful sound I have ever heard from a child. I sobbed and turned away so no one could see me crying. I still had a grip on his tiny arms while I was trying to wipe my tears on my shoulder or my arm, but all I could do was wipe away my tears on my coworker's scrubs. By this time she had gotten the IV, no problem, and was totally in control of what had been an uncontrollable situation, for me at least. She was taping down the IV and putting a mesh over his arm so he couldn't yank it out again, and she looked down at me, somewhat puzzled, and asked, "You never miss. What happened and . . . are you crying?" I told her I was just "having one of those days" and told her to just finish up with the damned IV. After a few more minutes, she saw I needed a break and offered to switch with me if I wanted to go to the other unit and take her adult patient, but I said I could finish out the day, thanks.

I finally pulled it together and finished up the day, and Awuas didn't pull out anything else, at least not during my shift. He eventually healed after multiple skin grafts and his uncle, whom he had been asking for, did finally come forward to take him home. Even though it's now been more than seven years, I can still see that little boy's precious face and hear those cries . . . and I hope his future is better than what he has already experienced. I do know many of my counterparts, seeing the fate of these innocent children in war zones, have applied for and been granted adoption of little ones they've treated. Awuas deserves nothing less than a happy childhood. If only wishing could make it so.

—Army Maj. Virginia Vardon-Smith, ICU Nurse

Every long-term relationship has a few flare-ups now and then. Whether it's newlyweds still learning about each other, best friends for life, or fathers and sons, it's inevitable they won't always agree. Hell, it's possible they won't always like each other, but if the relationship is worth maintaining, it will require tolerance, compromise, and maybe even a little tough love.

A True Test of Friendship

There are numerous physical wounds warriors endure as a direct result of their service. The wounds are evident with someone in a wheelchair—paralyzed from the impact of an improvised explosive device, missing a limb, disfigured or scarred from exposure to explosives. It is easy to look at them and know with certainty their lives and those of their loved ones are forever impacted by the injuries of war.

But what about all those wounded soldiers who come back home physically looking the same as when they left? They suffer equally with the unseen wounds of war—their damage is to the soul. When they have faced a traumatic event where they felt their life was in danger, and their sense of safety and trust is lost, it is a completely reasonable response to experience posttraumatic stress-related symptoms.

After an event soldiers may initially have trouble getting to sleep, have bad dreams, feel disconnected from others—not wanting to call home or hang out with their buddies—experience anxiety, or feel emotionally numb, giving the appearance they do not care about anything or anyone.

Most will process these emotions over the days or weeks following a traumatic event and the symptoms will alleviate. Some are impacted so significantly by their exposure—or repeated exposures—to combat that they develop posttraumatic stress (PTS). Soldiers might refuse to deal with their emotions surrounding the fearful memories by avoiding anything that might remind them of the event. This disconnection will often exacerbate and prolong the symptoms. In therapy a goal is to help them explore the memories and connect them to the intense emotions so they can become unstuck.

Some of these avoidance symptoms might seem obvious—a soldier has a panic attack in a crowded mall because he feels overwhelmed by the

Some wounds are evident—someone in a wheelchair, missing a limb, disfigured, or scarred from explosives. Many more have invisible wounds of war—damage to the soul. ARMY PHOTO

activity around him and helpless without a weapon to defend himself and his comrades to track everything around him that might be a threat, so he avoids crowds.

There are endless examples of how such symptoms can play out based on the person and the traumatic event, and that is where it can be difficult to identify and treat such symptoms.

I had an infantry soldier coming in many years ago for PTS treatment. It took several sessions to figure out one of his triggers for panic attacks and anger outbursts was hunger pains. It turned out one time his squad was outside the wire on a mission longer than anticipated and they did not have enough food. They were all starving and focused on the hunger pains when they became engaged in a firefight with the enemy.

Eventually we realized he connected that firefight with any current hunger pains, and without even realizing the mind-body connection his symptoms worsened with the physical signs of hunger.

I wish this was the only combatant I've worked with in dealing with PTSD, but in my many years of working for the Army in behavioral health, I have heard from various soldiers who have shared their stories with me, either as a counselor or as a friend: infantrymen engaged in firefights, truck drivers hitting IEDs, combat medics tending to wounded soldiers while on the battlefield, mechanics on recovery missions having to tow vehicles where soldiers have been mortally wounded, soldiers working in the makeshift morgues.

I've also talked with behavioral health providers going to remote areas to process recent traumatic events, leaders reflecting on and sometimes questioning decisions they made in battle, medics who could not save a comrade, a young man having his best friend die in his arms; it's a long list of deeply personal stories and they have all touched me deeply. It takes immense bravery for a soldier to not only come in and admit they need some help, but to share their deepest wounds with a stranger.

Then I had a realization: While all these stories have touched me, there was one patient who stood out from the others, who has had the greatest impact on me. It was not a patient who had come to me for treatment; it was a good friend. At work I am used to, and try to be comfortable in, dealing with trauma. I have worked in an Army behavioral clinic since the start of the war and have been afforded exceptional training opportunities and have been taken under the wings of phenomenal mentors.

At the start of my career, the number of active duty providers staffing the clinics was far greater than it is now, and I quickly acquiesced to the Army culture, regulations, and behavioral medicine under the tutelage of some fantastic men and women in uniform. I felt confident in my abilities to assess, diagnosis, and treat soldiers coming into the clinic for various behavioral health issues, but certainly over time trauma-related issues would take center stage.

But when I began to recognize certain signs and symptoms with a close friend, I was in unfamiliar territory, on the other side of the desk and out of my element; I was dealing with PTS in my personal life as opposed to someone seeking my professional assistance in the structured setting of a clinic. Ray was a career soldier returning from another twelve-month combat tour—his fourth time to the Middle East. When I say career, I mean he lived for the Army; it was his priority and central focus. He was prior enlisted, now a seasoned officer, and often took jobs that focused less on career progression and more on his desire to keep close to soldiers. Between assignments, training schools, and multiple deployments, he had not spent more than a year in any one place in over a decade. He took pride in his ability to "cut anchor" as he described it and start anew somewhere else.

Like many soldiers, he accepted the lifestyle of the Army and would readily go where told to meet his mission. For the ordinary person this might seem like a mini–life crisis to endure every year; but he coped with it and quickly adjusted to his environment, got his needs met, and made the best of every situation—resiliency is a key ingredient to success in the military. But what are the emotional costs and the impact on one's personal life over time with such continual change?

At first glance it was easy to focus on his bright smile, firm handshake, squared away appearance, and exuberance—all the traits of a confident and strong leader. He took pride in his career and knew he was good at what he did. He enjoyed leading/mentoring soldiers, solving complex problems, and being challenged, both physically and mentally. One exceptional quality that stood out to me was his ability to engender respect from his soldiers; no matter how busy, his door was always open and he had an uncanny ability to relate, maybe because he was prior enlisted himself. I watched his interactions with some of the soldiers and heard them speak about him with trust and respect. An injured infantryman related one particularly revealing incident: One day Ray was engaged in conversation when the young private walked past him, but Ray stopped talking to shake his hand and ask him how he was doing. The infantryman truly appreciated that kind of respect.

Trouble sleeping, having bad dreams, feeling disconnected from others, not wanting to call home or hang out with buddies, feeling emotionally numb, experiencing anxiety . . . all signs of posttraumatic stress. *MARINE* MAGAZINE PHOTO

Ray seemed to put high value on the needs of his soldiers, and not only had an appreciation for the role of behavioral health, but had no problems encouraging soldiers to use our services. On the surface he seemed fully engaged and had his life together. His house, car, and office were meticulously clean and organized; everything had its place including his multiple awards perfectly aligned on his walls. When engaged in conversation he was attentive, charismatic, and always had something of value to contribute. When out with friends he was usually full of life, intent on a good time. I have spoken to mutual friends of ours who deployed and spent time with him and the consensus was always that he was a great soldier, an upstanding man, willing to mentor, who shared his vast knowledge and gave his time and energy to help others, always. He was the type of person people often wanted to be around—fun, casual, friendly, easy to talk to.

There was a catch with Ray though—once you had his attention he was all these things, but it was usually on his terms, if and when he would do something. He tended to isolate often, almost as if to conserve his energy so when he did interact with other people he could be "on his game" or engaging. He enjoyed socializing but it did not come easy to him anymore and required more energy. He admitted to liking being on his own, and it took a lot for him to come out of his shell. He liked adventure, things that brought a rush of adrenaline, not uncommon among those who have served in combat. When talking about skydiving, scuba diving, or racing he would say, "I love the vibration of the steering wheel, the quiet beauty of the ocean, and the wind in my face. They make me feel." They also were things he could do with little to no interaction with others.

Those same friends who valued his companionship also noted it was challenging at times to get a response from him, and that he was consistently late or delayed making plans—something I have found to be a challenge in our friendship as well. He used to say he was not on a clock because he'd had rigid time constraints on deployments, so in his personal life he was going to do what he wanted, when he wanted to do it. If people did not like how he communicated, well "too bad."

Over time he has improved, and I don't believe his "I don't care" attitude is reflective of his true feelings. I used to ask myself, "Is this a display of selfish behaviors as a result of not wanting or feeling the need to be

He would return home seeing other soldiers and Marines at the airport greeted by loved ones, while he was alone due to two divorces and distancing himself from his own child. MARINE CORPS PHOTO

accountable to anyone? Or are his behaviors a result of ineffective coping strategies as he tries to manage the internal stressors which leave him feeling overwhelmed?"

When Ray returned from his most recent deployment, he had been through two divorces in addition to other failed relationships over his time in the Army. His wife filed for divorce during his deployment, and he would return home seeing other soldiers at the airport greeted by loved ones, while he was alone.

During deployments some soldiers disconnect from home life as an attempt to minimize the pain of missing loved ones, so when a soldier gets home they are then faced with trying to process a year's worth of life events that have happened during their absence.

Ray had a child and other family who he had not seen in three years. He heard complaints about his lack of visits home and minimal communication. It was not that he did not want to see his child—this was very painful for him—but his avoidance of anything that created anxiety or uncomfortable emotions was often a driving force behind his decisions.

After many failed attempts to communicate about visitation with his ex-wife, he could no longer endure the stress of dealing with her.

In trying to remain in control of his emotions, he would choose to avoid those situations in which he felt he could lose control of his emotions and be reactive. I asked him how he could function in a war zone but not be able to deal with his ex-wife, and he quickly responded, "War is easy for me, dealing with her is too hard." It became easier for him not to feel any emotions about it rather than feel the constant pain and guilt of the absence.

This was not the first time I had heard an active duty father tell me it was not that they didn't want to be part of their children's lives; rather it was easier for them to not see them at all versus seeing them sporadically and having to continually say goodbye, or the ultimate slap in the face, seeing their children call another man Dad.

While Ray loved and missed his mother, the more he put off visiting home the harder it became to do. He did not want to deal with his large family demanding his time—pulling him in different directions, asking questions about deployments, or lecturing about his long absences or life choices—so he simply avoided going home. The one consistently positive and structured part of his life was his Army career. But shortly after his return he learned he did not make the promotion list, just another blow in a series of disappointments. He was now faced with retirement earlier than expected. He had ambivalent feelings about this, as he expressed a desire to take a new career path he felt was more aligned with his religious views and desire to help others. He was tired of the many deployments and was ready to move on to something else, but the Army was all he knew and a large portion of his self-identity and self-worth was tied to his career; so when he was passed over for promotion, he felt another betrayal from the entity that he had given himself to at the cost of other areas of his life.

He was now struggling to juggle multiple and significant life events at the same time—the transition back from overseas deployment, his wife leaving him, disappointment with his career, and now forced retirement. Ray said he felt like a boxer knocked out and laying on the mat after taking so many hits, unable to move. Only after several months was he

After multiple deployments and the hardships of saying goodbye, unlike others who couldn't wait to get home and be with loved ones, he figured it was easier just to build walls and shut out everyone.
AIR FORCE PHOTO

able to get up, still disoriented and trying to regain his balance. When problems would arise in his personal life, he could just bury himself further in his work and find validation from his accomplishments, but now this was no longer an option. He had to try and shift gears and engage in the process of retirement when he was struggling just to manage in light of all the other stressors.

Being resilient and having a history of surviving in challenging situations, he tried to keep his head above water, a true test of his inner strength. He found ways to stay busy with travel and began to think about career options. Normally he was very guarded with his personal life and emotions, but his usual coping strategies were not effective this time and he began to look to other ways to cope, which included trying to establish some friendships and become more open about his life.

I could tell that at the very least he was struggling with an adjustment disorder—showing symptoms of anxiety and depression directly related to significant events occurring in his life. He had difficulty falling and staying asleep, often having nightmares and feeling restless. He felt a loss of interest in many activities, or Ray would just go through the motions of doing them to appear "normal" without really finding much joy in the task.

He would use escapist behaviors to either physically remove himself from his problems (by traveling) or mentally escaping (through watching movies or researching various topics of interest that had nothing to do with situations in his life). He had guilt about not seeing his son and mom. He would hyper-focus on a task to the extent of ignoring anything else around him, or he would jump from one thing to the next. His appetite was so low he would usually just eat one meal per day. He was emotionally numb and had a hard time expressing an appropriate range of emotions about situations in his life, feeling overloaded and just shutting down and shutting everyone out. Ray would say, "I just have to take a knee and get away from the noise going on around me and clear my head; I don't know why everyone gets mad at me for that?"

The few times when he was able to open up and share his feelings, he was so emotionally drained he would often isolate himself for days. He would say that his various divergent negative or emotional memories were compartmentalized in his brain, and if he opened the doors and let the emotions out it was hard to get them back in, despite his efforts to control them. I believe his excessive need to clean and organize is yet another way he tried to control his emotions by controlling his environment. The fixation on tasks kept his mind preoccupied from unwanted thoughts and instead gave him something result-oriented to focus all his energy on. He would easily prioritize managing such tasks ahead of socializing because to do otherwise required emotions that only created anxiety.

One day I sat outside a restaurant where Ray and I had agreed to meet. As always he was late, but this time more so than usual. We would try to meet for lunch or dinner often to talk, and we enjoyed each other's company, because we had similar interests and generally got along well. I really appreciated the time he took to explain in more detail about the life of soldiering, of military history, and the toll of multiple deployments. He would share war movies and history lessons he used to train junior officers, and it really gave me some excellent perspective in working with soldiers.

Over time, I observed chronic deregulation of his affect; sometimes he was guarded and formal in his speech, taking care to say things just right, and he would speak about topics of interest making little to no mention of his issues at hand; other times he would openly share what was on his mind with great sincerity. Posttraumatic stress does not rob people of their emotions; it just makes them muted, harder to express,

Escapist behaviors became more frequent as he sought ways to distance himself from a myriad of issues. By volunteering for multiple deployments, he didn't have the time to deal with marital and family issues and financial burdens. ARMY PHOTO

and that can be painful to want to reach out but not feel they can, afraid to trust anyone—to feel vulnerable.

Our time together was usually enjoyable, but it was frustrating when he would often wait until the last minute to make plans; he seemed to have trouble committing to the simplest arrangements and was frequently late. The excuses were often similar—he had tasks to complete at home or work or got caught up in something that couldn't wait. I would not get angry, because I understood him well enough to know it was not personal; he truly was hyper-focused on whatever he was doing and seemed driven to complete his mission before moving on to anything else. When he would tell me a time, I would often just add fifteen minutes to it. One time he actually arrived for dinner earlier than me at one of his favorite restaurants, and upon my arrival he was already back outside and telling me it was too crowded and we should go someplace else. He definitely had a different demeanor when sitting in a familiar and less crowded environment than he did being in someplace new or busy. He could manage fine if he had to, but he was more focused on his surroundings and on edge when in a busier place.

Just as in war, he seemed to deal with immediacy, though he often realized there were consequences for his actions. He chose to think about the task at hand and nothing else mattered at that time; he would deal with any consequences later. I often wondered if when he canceled or was late for our meetings, if he wanted to avoid getting into any emotional conversations because he wasn't certain he could control his emotions, and so he just simply avoided interacting. If he could not control the situation, the way the game was played, he avoided it altogether.

I waited at the restaurant feeling completely invalidated, as if my time was of no significance and he could not even bother to let me know he would be a no-show. I called—no answer. I texted—no response. Thinking this was out of character for Ray to be so blatantly disrespectful, I began to worry.

I left him a message, asking him to call me and let me know what was going on. I began to imagine the worst and struggled with conflicting emotions of hurt that he would be so dismissive and fear that something must be wrong. I waited an hour before going home. It was a couple of hours later when Ray finally texted that he was fine, he just didn't feel like going out and needed "time alone" and wondered inquisitively why I could not understand that. For a moment I was relieved he was okay, but then I was consumed with frustration because he seemed to show no remorse and even wondered why it might have bothered me. Intellectually I was able to make the connection between his actions and what was starting to look like PTSD, based on the observations I made over many times we'd been together.

But, this was not work, and he was not one of my patients. This was a close friend and he was part of my life, and although I could clearly see the symptoms, I was having a difficult time separating emotions from logic. I realized as intelligent as he was, if he had difficulty sorting through his own emotions, how could he be empathetic with another person?

I was feeling like a disappointed and devalued acquaintance and not an understanding counselor trained to accept the daily fluctuations in his mood. I told myself they were not about our friendship or me, but were all about his struggles with PTSD. On the good days, the real Ray would prevail, but on other days, his PTSD was in charge. I was now seeing things from a more vulnerable position, as I pondered the complaints I have heard over the years from loved ones as they shared their struggle to figure out what was PTSD-related and what was disrespectful behavior that would need to be more directly addressed.

For Ray it was obvious his avoidance was the key to controlling his emotions and thereby mitigating the chances of feeling vulnerable or of being harmed. He would avoid people, places, situations, and topics of conversation that he considered triggers to more intense emotions. Control and avoidance became central themes in his life. He liked to travel and socialize, to an extent, so although he would put himself into less controlled environments, it was easy to tell he had a heightened sense of awareness, an acute alertness to his surroundings.

Based on his sharing and my observations, I knew some of his triggers but not all of them, making it harder to understand or even anticipate certain moods. I am sure, like many sufferers of PTSD, he was not even aware of all his triggers. I have noticed one of his triggers was also one of the very things he thrives on—change.

He liked routine, familiarity, organization, and structure and when that got disrupted he got anxious, creating a desire to regain control. This anxiety turned to adrenaline, which he thrived on, and he went on auto-pilot, setting his agenda and knocking out tasks.

He would respond to his inner dialogue, convincing himself that any future consequences would be better than dealing with any semblance of conflict and the ensuing emotions. He would let time pass and let emotions cool before he would reengage. Ray was a wounded soul, often a prisoner to his own inner conflicts and the inability to fully connect his emotions to his trauma.

I wondered early in our friendship if this was just Ray being selfish, not thinking about the feelings of others, just his own. However, I think in many instances it was his way of protecting people in his life, as he

Ray was the ideal officer, concerned about the welfare of his soldiers, and yet he couldn't take care of himself, or his family. ARMY PHOTO

did not want to risk exposing them to his poorly modulated emotions—dragging them into his personal war to get hurt by him or to be hurt himself. He was always thoughtful, uplifting, and supportive with me, never a cruel word, and possibly did not want to risk jeopardizing that established positive pattern of behavior by being around me when he was not feeling in control. However, he needed to learn that part of trust was knowing he did not always have to be "perfect" during an interaction for us to have a good friendship.

So how has all of this impacted my life? In multiple ways. Our friendship was a glaring reminder that no matter how much we know about something, there is always more to learn. When soldiers come into my office to discuss trauma-related issues, I feel more adept at helping them heal. Not just because of watching Ray's struggles with PTSD, but also the depth and breadth of knowledge he shared with me from his over twenty years of being a soldier.

45

His greatest desire is to have a positive impact on "Joe," and through his friendship and the time he spent educating me, he is absolutely having an impact on soldiers. Nobody else can explain someone else's feelings better than that person, but I think Ray's ability to articulate and share insights about some generalized feelings combat soldiers might share was extremely beneficial for me in sessions with younger soldiers as they tried to explain some of their experiences.

I also have new respect and understanding for the family and friends of PTSD sufferers—understanding the struggles they face setting boundaries, validating their feelings, redefining relationships, and navigating their own sea of emotions. There is no simple formula, as every situation is unique.

I don't define Ray by a label of PTSD. I readily see past that to the man I am privileged to call one of my best friends. He's a good man, a loyal friend, a trusted confidant, a religious mentor, and someone who has brought much joy to my life; it just so happens he has PTSD.

No friendship is perfect, and we face challenges that can either create distance between us or act as building blocks to make our friendship stronger.

I have a friend who is paralyzed from the waist down due to the impact of an IED blast in Afghanistan. I would never turn my back on our friendship just because of his war injuries, so why would I turn my back on Ray just because he returned from war with different injuries? Should he be alienated for honorably serving his country and as a result not being the exact same person he was before he left? This is all new territory for him, trying to push past his discomfort and work on relationships in his life so he can enjoy closeness with others and feel connected . . . something he's avoided in the past.

He resists the urge to "cut anchor" when difficulties arise and instead tries to work past them. He realizes relationships take effort and while some might lead to disappointment, others may be well worth it, and he is slowly and cautiously opening up to the idea of taking that risk.

The boundaries seem more clear to me now; as long as effort continues to be made on both of our ends and the positives of the friendship outweigh the negatives, then it continues to be worth it to me. I have learned to give him space and not take it as a personal slight when he is not responding to me in a manner or timeframe I would prefer. I find that when I only bring issues to his attention that really bother me, he is very receptive and I almost always notice his effort to resolve the issue. Even if he does not speak of it, I see it in his actions. Even though he might not communicate to the extent I like to, I think he appreciates that in me.

I have learned to appreciate people who speak very little and still express much in what they say and do. We both continue to learn for and challenge each other. Ray has also been willing to seek help for behavioral health, something he encouraged soldiers to do but he personally resisted until more recently, once likening it to "unburying my dead dog." He is a lifelong friend and I would never turn my back on him. Recently he sent me this quote from C. S. Lewis: "Friendship is unnecessary, like philosophy, like art. . . . It has no survival value; rather it is one of those things that give value to survival."

—Laura Gregory, Licensed Independent Social Worker

Just when they think they've seen it all, another bizarre casualty comes in, like none before. For Air Force Maj. Trish Hayden, her unforgettable wounded warrior was a young Army soldier with a "slight headache" on a medevac flight out of Iraq.

"My Head Hurts a Little"

In the summer of 2007, I was on my first deployment to a war zone, Balad Air Base in Iraq. I had joined the Air Force in 2003 and had never been deployed until then; it was also my first assignment as a nurse with a critical care air transport team, CCATT. To be honest, I was scared of entering a war zone and afraid I was not good enough to take care of our nation's wounded heroes. My respiratory therapist, who deployed with me, was not only an experienced CCATT member; he was also my friend who would be by my side the entire deployment.

My Air Force Reserve unit, the 920th Aeromedical Staging Squadron, was based at Patrick Air Base in Florida. I was part of CCATT at that unit, which was basically a flying intensive care unit. The teams consisted of three highly trained medical personnel: a critical care physician, a critical care nurse, and a critical care respiratory therapist. Our primary job was to fly the critically wounded warriors out of country.

We had flown maybe ten missions out of Iraq when we were given an especially difficult mission. It was midday on July 3, 2007. I was in my PT gear walking around base when my pager went off. I called in to the Aeromedical Evacuation Operations office to see what was up and they said my team, and an aeromedical evacuation (AE) team, was being alerted immediately for an emergency mission. When I asked what it was they simply said to put on my flight suit, grab my go bag, and head on in and the details would be given once we got there. When we got to the trailer, we received our medical briefing. An Army sergeant had been stabbed in the head by an Iraqi insurgent, and we had to fly him directly to the States because of his critical condition. This was only the third time an aeromedical flight had flown from Iraq directly to the States. Normally, the missions flew from downrange into Ramstein Air Base in Germany, and then another team would take them to the States after the patients were further stabilized. But due to his injury the sergeant had to go directly to the States rather than the usual route.

It was not until six months later when I found out the entire story about Sergeant Powers, from the man himself, which I will explain later.

Our critical care team traveled with 750 pounds of medical equipment along with our personal belongings . . . and snacks for the ride, which were often consumed just to occupy our time, or to offset our nervous energy. We gathered everything up, received our intelligence briefing, signed out our weapons, and then headed to the hospital to package our patient for the flight.

Sergeant Powers was still in surgery when we got there, so we got a report from the nurse and the emergency room physician about his condition. He had been stabbed in the head while detaining an Iraqi insurgent. When he was brought in to the ER by his unit via Humvee, he was still awake and talking. At first they wanted us to fly him with the knife still lodged in his head, but after consulting a neurosurgeon back in the States they decided to remove it before flying him out.

Technology played a major role in Sergeant Powers's surgery that

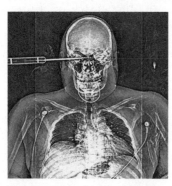

He was stabbed in the head by an Iraqi insurgent. CAT scans pinpointed the exact location of the blade and would show any potential damage to the brain.
AIR FORCE PHOTO

day. CAT scans were taken of his brain to find the exact location of the blade and to see if there was any additional damage that could pose issues during the removal process. The CAT scans were emailed to a neurosurgeon at Bethesda Hospital, who was actually driving home from work at the time. The surgeon received a phone call letting him know he would be getting the scans soon and the surgeons downrange, in Iraq, needed his assistance and guidance on how to remove the knife safely. The surgeon pulled over, opened up his laptop, and logged on to his Hotmail account. He opened the scans from his email, reviewed them right there on the side of the road, and instructed the surgeons on how to remove the knife safely.

The procedure was done with only one minor issue and the knife was removed. Initially, the knife was given to me to take back to the States and give to Sergeant Powers's family. However, after security forces got involved, they took the knife from me and eventually "processed" it and mailed it to Powers a few months later.

Once Powers was out of surgery, we packaged him up for the flight and made our way to the aircraft, a C-17. The flight was going to be approximately fifteen hours, and we were scheduled for two midair refuelings. Since we were going to the States they gave us another patient, a nineteen-year-old soldier who had been shot in the neck during a reconnaissance mission. He was critical as well, and since we had plenty of room we got to take him directly home too. Sergeant Powers and the other soldier were the only two patients on the flight.

The first few hours were uneventful. Both patients were stable, but it was Sergeant Powers I was worried about. He had major surgery to his head. They removed a piece of his skull to compensate for any swelling of the brain that could have occurred. He also had a "bolt" in his head, which was placed so we could measure the pressure in his head (intracranial pressure) during the flight. If this elevated it could pose huge problems for him. His brain could herniate and cause irreparable damage.

Fifteen hours is a long time to be awake, taking care of two critically wounded heroes, and this was after we had already been up for more than ten hours prior to takeoff. But we had an amazing team and the aeromedical evacuation crew was the best

Once he got out of surgery—to remove the knife from his head—he and another soldier were prepped for the flight to Andrews Air Base stateside. Normally critically injured patients in Iraq and Afghanistan would be flown to Ramstein Air Base in Germany, where they would then be transported to nearby Landstuhl Hospital. AIR FORCE PHOTO

of the best. They hung in there with us and helped us any way they could to take care of our patients. It was a routine flight, but it was shaping up to be the perfect situation for the perfect, potential storm.

Halfway through the flight, we needed to have our first midair refueling. (At the end of the flight, we found out from the flight crew we actually missed our first "stop" for the refueling and we had only refueled once.) During that refueling the plane was bouncing around a lot. I have never felt anything like that before in my life. I was at Sergeant Powers's side, with the AE nurse holding his litter, trying to prevent it from bouncing up and down. My respiratory therapist was at the other litter, with one of the techs, doing the same. All of us were hanging on just to keep from getting tossed around like rag dolls.

As we were getting bounced and jostled, I noticed Sergeant Powers's intracranial pressure was rising. Any number less than 20 millimeters of mercury (mmHg) was considered okay (15 or less is optimal), and his was ranging between 15 and 18. As the plane continued to plow through turbulence, during the refueling, his number was climbing . . . 18 . . . 19 . . . 21. I started to think "oh shit." So first I did manual checks on Powers. I made sure his neck collar was not too tight. Then I made sure his head was midline and I checked his pupils to make sure they were not dilated. (If they were dilated, then we were in big trouble!)

Everything checked out okay, but then his blood pressure and heart rate started going up. The only thing I could do was increase his sedation and hopefully it would relax him a little bit more.

After a quick push of more sedation medication and increasing his hourly rate, Sergeant Powers's intracranial pressure started to come back to normal after maxing at 25 mmHg. His heart rate and blood pressure came down as well. (Later I found out that Powers was afraid of flying, even though he was a Ranger in the Army and was being trained to be a jumper. After that rollercoaster ride of a flight, I wasn't a big fan either.)

We finally landed at Andrews Air Force Base the morning of July 4 after more than a fourteen-hour flight. What an amazing feeling it was to be able to transport a couple of wounded warriors home on Independence Day. The ambulance picked us up on the flight line, and we dropped both patients off at Bethesda Hospital in Maryland. We never thought we would see or hear from Sergeant Powers again.

Six months after the historic flight, both teams—the aeromedical evacuation crew and our critical care air transport team—received a call from Air Mobility Command. Since the flight was so historic, with an amazing outcome and the use of a true total force, we were all invited to an annual conference where we would be recognized for the mission. This is where we heard the full story of Sergeant Powers's injury.

The story began with Sergeant Powers and his unit. They were out performing a reconnaissance mission when they were attacked by Iraqi insurgents. They got the situation under control, and Powers was standing over an insurgent with his rifle aimed down at him while he was detaining him. Without warning the insurgent reached into his boot, pulled out a knife, swung his arm up, and stabbed Sergeant Powers in the right side of his head. Powers did not move. He maintained his position without even realizing what had happened.

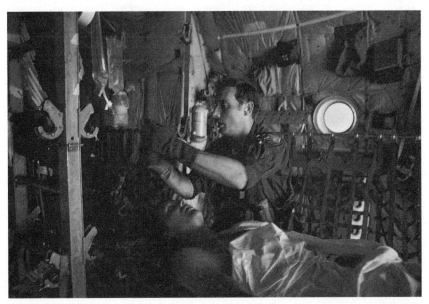

During the flight from Iraq to Andrews Air Base, the transport plane encountered turbulence during a midair refueling, and his blood pressure and heart rate increased to dangerous levels. DOD PHOTO

One of his buddies walked up to him and said, "Hey Dan, you know you have a knife sticking out of your head?" At first he didn't believe him until he looked sideways at his head, and saw something shiny sticking out from just to the periphery of his right eye. One of the other soldiers took over for him and they made him sit down. Powers was talking to them as a Humvee drove him to the hospital at Balad Air Base, Iraq. That is where we came in.

At the conference, they walked all of us on stage, highlighting the use of a total force. First the Army folks from Sergeant Powers's unit came out. Then it was the Air Force active duty folks from the hospital at Balad.

Next was the aeromedical evacuation crew from the Air National Guard who was on the flight with us. Then our critical care air transport team, which included our active duty Air Force doctor and our respiratory therapist and myself, both of us Air Force Reservists. Next, came the Navy neurosurgeon who had pulled off the road to look at the scans on his computer, and talked the surgeons downrange through the surgery. Then finally, out came Sergeant Powers and his wife, Trudy, which was a total surprise for all of us on stage. We had no idea he was going to be there. We had heard he just had surgery to put a titanium plate in his head and his surgeon would not allow him to come to the conference. But, as miracles can happen, he was able to be there and let me tell you there was not a dry eye in the house as Dan and his wife walked across the stage and gave each and every one of us a hug. What an amazing moment, personally and professionally!

We got to talk to Dan and Trudy for a long time, and that is when we heard the entire story from him and also learned he was afraid of flying. At that point it finally made sense why all of his numbers elevated during the midair refueling and why the additional sedation worked. They still have the knife that was lodged in his head, but Trudy keeps it in a drawer and says she still can't look at it.

To this day I still keep in touch with Dan and Trudy. I am blessed to have them in my life and to be able to call them my dear friends. That day in Balad, I think possibly God had a plan when my team was alerted for the mission to bring Dan home. It was to bring two wonderful people into my life. Dan is a brave soldier, an amazing husband, and a dear friend.

Six months after an Iraqi insurgent stabbed him in the head with a knife, Sgt. Dan Powers met Maj. Trish Hayden, one of the critical care air transport team members who cared for him during a fourteen-hour flight. TRISH HAYDEN'S PERSONAL PHOTO

He is still in the Army doing incredible things. Since his injury he has deployed two more times, once to Afghanistan and once to South Korea. He has also become a certified jumper for the Army, though he's still not very fond of flying. He is a true American hero, a courageous soldier, and someone we should all hope to be like someday. I am still in the Air Force Reserves, performing my duties as a critical care air transport team nurse. Transporting critically wounded warriors home is an extremely rewarding job. I get to bring troops home to their loved ones and give them the chance at recovery, or give the families a chance to say goodbye and maybe have some closure. I truly have the best job in the world!!

—Maj. Trish Hayden, Critical Care Air Transport
Team Nurse with the Air Force Reserve 920th
Aeromedical Staging Squadron

When wounded warriors are brought in for emergency care, military doctors and nurses realize they're treating more than just another patient. They're someone's son or daughter, a husband or wife, a father or mother. They all have someone back home who cares.

A Proud Father

In 2004 I was a freshly minted second lieutenant deployed with the combat support hospital to Baghdad, Iraq. I worked in the intensive care unit where we took care of the wounded, both friend and foe. It was during this year-long deployment that one patient had a strong impact on me. In fact, he forever changed me, and I can't even remember his name.

I don't mean to come off as callous and uncaring, but I think every caregiver has a breaking point. After so many tears, so many body bags, and giving it your very best only to see them die so young, you become numb and just want to get through each day's shift. So, eventually you just see the wounds and no longer remember the names. Somehow it's easier if we don't know their names. I haven't decided yet if writing this is going to be therapeutic for me or just tear open old wounds that still haven't healed completely.

I don't think I ever knew his name, but he looked like "John" so I'll call him that. Tragically, he was much too young to be so close to dying, so maybe Johnny would be more appropriate. If you removed all the tubes and wires and IVs and monitors that kept him alive, there wouldn't be any obvious wounds, no traumatic injuries—that is except for a small wound to his cheek made by a sniper's bullet that had tunneled to his spine. It paralyzed him from the neck down, and now his body could no longer automatically tell his lungs to breathe.

During my assessment of John, I immediately saw that he was in a heightened state of fear. His eyes were wide-open and he seemed desperate to be anywhere else but where he was. He couldn't speak because he was on a ventilator to do all of his breathing for him. He could, however, blink his eyes. Since his cervical spine was severely damaged, he couldn't

No obvious wounds, except a small hole by his cheek made by a sniper's bullet that tunneled to his spine and left him paralyzed. ARMY PHOTO

move his head up and down or from side to side. Nodding a simple "Yes" or "No" to communicate just wasn't going to work.

I wanted to see what was causing him so much distress, so I wrote out the alphabet in big letters on a piece of paper and held it up to John's face so he could see. Then I took my pen and told him to blink when I got to the letter he wanted me to spell. I slowly moved my hand from left to right, line by line, on my makeshift communication tool. The first letter was "W." Then "I" and so on. He spelled out "WIFE" so then I said, "Yes, we will contact your wife and let her know you are here in the hospital, in Baghdad." I assumed that was what was troubling him, but he wanted to tell me something more. I picked up the paper again and we

He was paralyzed from the neck down, and even though he was going home earlier than planned, he would never get to hold his newborn baby. AIR FORCE PHOTO

slowly spelled out "B" then "A" until eventually John spelled out the word "BABY." "Did your wife just have a baby?" I asked him and John blinked vigorously. This time I was right.

So there we were, a new nurse in a combat zone still getting used to the distant rumble of explosions, with a young soldier lying helpless, now a quadriplegic, telling me his wife back home just had a baby. I was doing my best not to tear up in front of him and just focused on creating a calm environment for him. Even though he was paralyzed and couldn't feel much, he could certainly hear the chaos of the emergency room, and see all the monitors and bright lights and others passing by, all with a sense of urgency. I put my hand on John's head to try to comfort him. It was the only thing he could feel, and he obviously knew his situation was grim. Still, I did my best to keep him comfortable that night.

I was married without kids, so I had no idea what to tell this new father. He received some medications to help ease his anxiety and eventually he closed his eyes to sleep. By the next day, John was on a medevac plane headed home, wherever home was, and I have no idea what happened to him, but it doesn't take much to know he was facing enormous challenges. Today, as a father I now know why he was in such a state of panic. It was a soldier's love for his family. Even though he was paralyzed from the neck down, the only thing he thought about, the only thing that soldier cared about, was his wife and newborn child. It was an incredible act of selflessness. Sometimes when I hug my own children I close my eyes and think, "This one is for John, for that young soldier who can't wrap his arms around his own son or daughter." Through John I've learned to appreciate everything about life and treasure every moment with my family. Thank you John.

—Anthony Pansoy

Sometimes the compassion a doctor or nurse might feel for a critically injured combatant is tested, especially if that patient is an enemy prisoner of war who may have recently killed Americans . . . and wouldn't hesitate to do it again if given the opportunity.

The Iraqi Republican Guard was battle-tested after a ten-year war with Iran, and promised to destroy any Coalition forces who invaded their homeland. Total destruction did occur, as Saddam Hussein's military collapsed with barely a whimper, and the Highway of Death leading out of Kuwait was littered with Iraqi tanks, trucks, and anything else Iraqi soldiers could commandeer.
DEFENSE MEDIA PHOTO

Compassion for an Enemy Combatant

During the first Gulf War with Iraq, my combat support hospital (CSH) was partially set up fifty miles west of the Euphrates River valley. We preplanned and arranged our six identically stocked, side-by-side trauma tables with teams of three consisting of one doctor, one registered nurse, and one medic. The war practically ended as soon as it began, with minimal US casualties.

(During the buildup to Desert Storm, Iraq had one of the largest battle-tested armies in the world, and Saddam Hussein promised a lopsided victory. And the international press ate it up. In fact, it was a lopsided victory, as Coalition forces steamrolled the Iraqi Republican Guard, who had three options: die in a war they didn't believe in; surrender en masse—which thousands in fact did; or shed their uniforms, abandon their tanks and field guns, toss aside their tattered accoutrements of battle, and blend into the local population.)

As such, nearly all of our patients on this one particular shift were Iraqi soldiers. Pre-arrival reports came in through our leadership. Apparently, we were about to receive multiple enemy prisoners of war (EPWs) who had been injured in a firefight with Americans. These injured had laid in the desert for at least two days following the fight. Several of them lacked basic first-aid supplies, food, or water and had simply packed their wounds with sand to stop any bleeding. These soldiers, including their commanders, had no medical backup support whatsoever. They did their best with what they had, lacking basic supplies and appropriate clothing to stay warm and survive in the winter desert.

Co-located with a mobile surgical hospital, we covered the twelve-hour day shift of trauma patients being flown in, and they covered the twelve-hour night shift. This particular day, several Black Hawks hovered over our CSH carrying at least four to six patients each. Our six trauma beds were hopping with activity.

Three additional helicopters with three to four patients on board still needed to land. At least twelve more Iraqi casualties who needed medical attention waited on litters in the sand under multicolored homemade blankets. Our chief nurse and other hospital leaders were expertly triaging the wounded right outside the trauma tent door.

Most of our patients had gunshot wounds from head to toe mixed with full and partial amputations of all body limbs. An Iraqi soldier repeatedly yelled in English from his trauma bed, "I'm Catholic! I'm Catholic!" As Americans representing multiple religions, we busily continued with our immediate interventions for our patients. We looked at each other, shrugged our shoulders, and concluded that he wanted us to treat him better than the others.

My team finished with each patient then went to the next bed, and the next and the next. The orthopedic surgeon, medic, and I moved from bed to bed, trauma patient to trauma patient, stabilizing them then moving on.

A quiet, heavily bearded enemy prisoner of war was laid before us. A filthy but colorfully striped blanket covered his legs. His intensely furrowed brow revealed he was in severe pain but not verbalizing it. After removing the blanket I was startled to see the white bedsheet through his mangled and filleted left lower leg. He wasn't bleeding, even though he'd been injured at least two days prior. His traumatic injury looked like a clean dissection I'd seen in my high school biology lab. Bone fragments protruded from below his knee with striations of skin and muscle attached to his dangling foot.

The Iraqi combatants had few choices once the war began: die for a futile cause and a ruthless dictator; abandon their weapons and blend into the local civilian populace; or surrender. Thousands chose to surrender. Many were severely wounded, left in the desert to die. ROYAL SCOTS REGIMENT PHOTO

Our operating room was already full. The triage area was also full with "more severe" injuries waiting. Then, came the horrible realization that we were out of pain medication. No additional anesthesia was available to us. We had no idea when we could expect more because our supply line had been temporarily cut off. Still, our primary mission was to quickly stabilize these injured soldiers and get them on medevac flights to Saudi Arabia. We simply couldn't wait. There were still more helicopters that needed to land.

While our designated medical providers cared for the wounded, we appointed at least one-third of our medics to guard the other twenty to thirty surrendering Iraqi soldiers walking up to our hospital.

The orthopedic doctor decided what was left of this man's leg must be removed. His leg was floppy and twisted and could not be reattached. We didn't speak Arabic and he didn't speak English. Nobody in the busy trauma area, whether American or Iraqi, knew how to translate. The doctor told me to help sit him up so we could have a "conversation" about

The Black Hawks were loaded with injured combatants—enemy prisoners of war—left on the battleground for days without care. For the staff at the combat support hospital, their role was not to take sides, but to treat the patients brought to them. AIR FORCE PHOTO

what was going to happen. I assisted him to a sitting position while the surgeon "spoke" to him in makeshift gestures and sign language. We conveyed to him that his leg, or what was left of it, must be removed. The man nodded affirmatively without emotion. He leaned on me while I laid him back down.

We prepared the instruments for amputation. As the surgeon began, I cradled the soldier's head and upper body on my arm while he yelled and I silently felt tears rise up in my eyes. American soldiers on our staff standing by watched, stunned by the emotionally traumatic event taking place before them. The leg was removed by a scalpel. His lower leg bones were already broken in multiple areas, so there was no need to use a surgical saw. There was also no need to hold him down. He didn't fight us. He understood and stoically bore the pain. I wondered about the degree of pain this man had already endured in his past. When the doctor finished, I wrapped the enemy soldier's new stump.

Being so acutely aware of his religious and gender beliefs, I felt I had treated him with the utmost respect and dignity. He allowed me, an American woman, to touch and care for him in those few moments without any resistance or hostility. He didn't push me away. He accepted the gesture of support and nodded "yes" as he looked at me when it was all over. I interpreted the nod as a thank you.

We looked at each other, eyes locked, after experiencing such a traumatic event. I was so sorry we couldn't help him with his pain. I tilted my head, touched his hair and face, and tried to convey my sorrow. On a human-to-human level, regardless of EPW status,

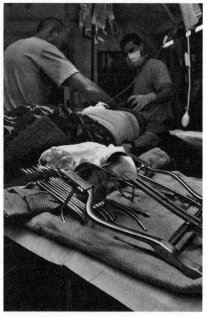

Surgical tools weren't needed this time. The man's leg was removed with just a scalpel. AIR FORCE PHOTO

religious beliefs, or gender differences, he and I understood each other. In an instant he was taken away for a short recovery and then transport out of the country. My team moved to the next trauma table, the next patient. There were several who were wounded with similar amputations.

I did an about-face to the bed behind me to treat the only American soldier brought in that day. The pilots told us he was alive when they picked him up, but he was pulseless when they put him on our trauma bed. The medic started CPR. After lifting up both of his sleeves only to find both of his hands missing, I continued looking for a good vein to start an IV. I momentarily thought about the other soldier who had just departed, then quickly switched my full attention to this young soldier who also had multiple shrapnel wounds over his chest, neck, and jaw. The pilots guessed he mistakenly picked up an exploding booby trap.

Over the next few days we continued to see patients, mostly enemy combatants. We treated a few civilians, a mother and daughter with gunshot wounds who were caught in the crossfire. They stayed for several days. An older gentleman, a member of their family, stayed outside the door of the tent where the mother and daughter were admitted. The man sat outside the tent all day and a few nights, rarely going in to see them. The mother was later discharged while the daughter was flown to Saudi Arabia for continued care. I continued to think and wonder about the man with the amputated leg. How was he doing? Where was he? How was he being treated?

"We looked at each other, eyes locked, after experiencing such a traumatic event. I was so sorry we couldn't help him with his pain. I tilted my head, touched his hair and face, and tried to convey my sorrow. On a human-to-human level, regardless of EPW status, religious beliefs, or gender differences, he and I understood each other." NAVY PHOTO

Our critical care area and operating room were the only parts of the hospital that were set up. We slept on cots outside for two days. After the mass casualties subsided, we packed our supplies and headed out of Iraq to Saudi Arabia. On that deployment we never set up our hospital again for patient care. The war had ended just as quickly as it started. Before leaving Saudi Arabia we opened our hospital supplies, cleaned them, repacked them for travel, and flew home. A few days later, when I finally had a chance to reflect on what had happened, I wept, thinking of that "one" patient, who endured an amputation without any available offering of relief. Even today, I think of him off and on . . . it's more than two decades later and my throat still hurts when I write this. I wonder where he is, what happened to him during this life? Technically, he may have been an enemy combatant, but to me, he was a patient who needed our care. I gave him my best and I hope he's always known that, even today.

—Cheryl L. Brown, Registered Nurse

The battle for Fallujah has quickly been etched in the glorious annals of Marine Corps history, right up there with Iwo Jima. Even prior to the battle, the casualty count was expected to be as high as 30 to 40 percent, but the insurgents using this Iraq city as a stronghold had to be exterminated, no matter the cost. This is the story of just two of our brave young Marines who fought there.

Two Hellish Days in Fallujah

Toward the end of our deployment in Iraq in 2004, I was a Navy corpsman and had been pulled back to the main battalion aid station for a short break from front-line duty, during the second assault on Fallujah during Operation Iraqi Freedom II. (The first assault had been in April of that year.) I was a Navy petty officer second class and had been with my battalion longer than most, having extended my stay. Since many of our other corpsmen were new to combat, my experience was going to count, and in combat that means saving lives.

After more than two years, I knew almost everyone in the battalion, so in a way I considered them all "my guys," and most of them knew me and knew they could count on me, even in the worst of firefights.

Fallujah in Iraq was a historic battle for the US Marines who fought there. It was brutal and deadly . . . for both sides. MARINE CORPS PHOTO

"With all the blood and dirt, it was hard to recognize him, that it was Smittie . . .
I just turned off my emotions . . . I couldn't let them cloud what I had to do."
MARINE CORPS PHOTO

We were at the aid station when one of the Marines came up to me.
Smittie and I had joined the battalion at around the same time and I had
been his senior line corpsman for almost two years. Even though I was
nearly ten years older than him, we knew each other well and he kind of
looked at me like a big brother, always asking for my advice. Should he do
this, should he stay in the military, etc. He was a good kid, even if he did
tease me about being so "old."

He had gotten a fairly nasty leg infection and was sent back to the
rear to rest and had now recovered, so he was itching to get back to his
company, but he needed medical clearance first. I asked if he was feeling
better, checked him out, took a few vitals, and jotted down some notes.
He seemed fine so I talked to the battalion surgeon, who said if I thought
he was good then that was good enough for him. I told Smittie he was
good to go, cleared for duty, and told him to be safe out there. He caught
a ride with his company gunny sergeant, who was driving back out to the
company. Smittie was a typical Marine; he just wanted to get back to his

brothers, who were battling the insurgents in one of the bloodiest missions of the war with Iraq.

That night we lay down, trying without much luck to sleep, with occasional shots going off from a C-130 gunship circling overhead, firing howitzer rounds on targets it picked up close by, in Fallujah. Like the steady rumble of thunder, those explosions from "Basher" become very comforting, whereas the silence is more discomforting than anything. Personally those rare occasions of total silence were unnerving for me.

The next day we received a call about incoming casualties, two gunshot wounds, one with a cricheotomy—a small tube placed through the cricothyroid membrane, to allow the patient to breathe. Soon after the call, they rolled in and there was blood everywhere, and some of the other Marines were crying and yelling at me, "It's Smith doc, it's Smittie." With all the blood and dirt, it was hard to recognize him, that it was Smittie, the Marine I had just cleared for duty the day before.

At first I just turned off my emotions; I couldn't let them cloud what I had to do or I'd go crazy. "Okay, let's work on him," I said. He'd been shot in the head but was still alive, unresponsive but he still had a pulse and was breathing. His brain matter was exposed in front. The battalion surgeon worked on him for ten minutes while I called for a medical evacuation helicopter, ran the quarter-mile in full combat gear down to the landing zone (LZ) and marked it, then rushed back to get the patient down there and on the bird, a CH-46.

We got him on board and strapped in and briefed the corpsman accompanying the helicopter. I just remember seeing Smittie as he left, still alive but it didn't look good. I was thinking to myself I should have kept him back for an extra day. If only, and that was a big "if," but I couldn't beat myself up about it. I put it away. The flight to the forward operating base hospital was only ten minutes, but two hours later we got word that he had died en route. Too young, just married a year prior, and his wife had gotten pregnant just before we left the States.

No time to mourn though. The next day we got another call about a Marine with a gunshot wound to the head, same company. It was like a repeat of the day before, and soon after the call they arrived, with blood

"The flight to the forward operating base hospital was only ten minutes, but two hours later we got word that he had died en route." MARINE CORPS PHOTO

everywhere, but this time it was Smittie's best friend. The two of them were always together, always in trouble together, best buds, and now he was shot in the head, just like Smittie. The round had entered just under his Kevlar and tore out part of the frontal skull, exposing the brain. He was unresponsive but had a lot stronger vital signs than Smittie.

I felt like I had been kicked right in the chest. It just wasn't fair, and it hurt like hell, but we still had a job to do; we had to save him. I remember running down to the landing zone again, and there were incoming mortar rounds and I was thinking we might not be able to get him out by helicopter due to the hot LZ, so we might have to transport him by ground, which takes longer.

I called for casevac, marked the site, and the bird came in. Those Marine pilots are great. We got him to the LZ, and as we were loading him onto the bird, he opened his eyes, saw me and said, "Doc, my head hurts like a mother!" I told him right there if he ever did that again I was going to kill him myself, though it wasn't a certainty he would make it.

That was ten years ago, and I can happily say he made it with no permanent damage—some say it's because all he had was marshmallow fluff between his ears. He is still in the Marines and is now a gunny sergeant. A few years ago we got together when one of our friends retired. We spent the night there on the beach, getting drunk and swapping war stories, remembering Smittie again.

I've never forgotten those two days in Iraq. Pure hell, especially losing Smittie. After just two days at the aid station, I couldn't wait to get back to my unit fast enough. I spent twenty-one days in Fallujah and the worst were those two days in the rear, helpless to do anything for Smittie. I didn't realize how bad it affected me until I came back from my second tour in Afghanistan. I started having dreams, panic attacks, and hyper-vigilance, which led to my medical discharge in 2012 for PTSD and TBI. Ten years and yet it still hurts inside, and I still think of Smittie and his wife, and their little girl who never got the chance to meet her dad, or ever know what a terrific guy he was.

—"Old Doc Donkey" (What all the troops called me.)

Often, at Landstuhl Regional Medical Center in Germany, patients arrive from war zones and depart within a few days, evacuated to military medical facilities stateside. For those medical personnel at Landstuhl, such as Lt. Col. Gail Fancher, their interactions with those patients in their care are brief, but often unforgettable.

Three Special Guys of the Many Patients at Landstuhl

I rounded every morning in the ICU at LRMC (Landstuhl Regional Medical Center) with the large gaggle of attendings, residents, and hospital staff. This particular morning, the lead trauma surgeon was commenting that he had been up the night before trying to save this patient's right leg. The soldier had been in an explosion caused by an unmounted improvised explosive device (IED) and had lost his left leg. His right leg had been injured in the explosion and fragments of his own femur had lacerated his right leg's blood supply. Although the downrange physicians had sewn the vein and initially saved the blood supply, the movement had jostled other bone fragments loose and had torn the fragile vessel, requiring the midnight surgical intervention.

Jonathan was resting quietly while the group discussed his care. As the group started to move to the next patient, I looked in at Jonathan one more time. This time we made eye contact and I decided to stop in and chat with him. I explained, "It's normal for the group to discuss each case in the morning. We aren't talking about you, but we are talking about you."

Raising his eyebrow and looking at me quizzically, he stated, "Either I'm under the influence or you don't make sense."

I laughed. "Probably a little of both. How are you doing?"

"Not bad," was his answer.

"I'm the aerovac doctor. It's my job to make sure you get home safe and sound."

He was polite and thanked me and I returned to the pack.

Jonathan was manifested to fly on the mission the next day. However, late that night he had trouble with his revascularization, and they

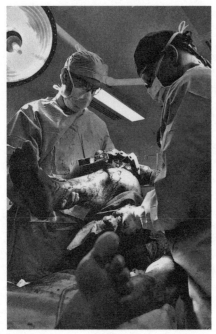

The trauma surgeon had been up the night before trying to save this patient's right leg. The soldier had been in an explosion caused by an IED. His right leg had been injured in the explosion and fragments of his own femur had lacerated his right leg's blood supply.
AIR FORCE PHOTO

went back to the operating room. He spent another two days with us in the ICU. The following day my arthritis was flaring so badly I needed my cane. As I puttered through the ICU with my cane, Jonathan called out to me. I peeked into his room and was met with an uneasy look.

"Are you okay?" He was concerned about me.

"Thank you, but don't worry, I'm just getting older," I joked.

He smiled and appeared relieved. Internally I paused. Here was a wounded warrior worried about me. What a kind heart this young man had. His parents would be proud. Again we manifested Jonathan for the next mission. A couple of hours later, though, the blood supply to Jonathan's leg clotted off and there was nothing to do but amputate. The right leg, the one the surgeons had tried to save, was no longer viable. The following morning I rushed to his side and gave him a hug.

"Oh, Jonathan, I'm so sad to hear of the loss of your leg."

He looked surprised and said, "Which one?"

"The one we've been trying to save," I stammered.

"Oh, it's okay. It hurt anyway," he replied. "Now I can get on with getting better!"

After that we chatted for a while. He was manifested again and this time I saw him off at the plane. As I reminisce about that day, I realize that Jonathan was named appropriately. His name means "gift of God," and he had definitely been my gift that day. He would be just fine.

———

After rounds in the ICU one morning I stopped in to see Lieutenant Lee. The LT was leading his men when he stepped on an IED and lost both legs. Lee was sitting up in the bed talking to his nurse when I peeked in the door.

"Come on in," invited the soldier.

"Hey. I'm the aerovac doctor. It's my job to make sure you get home safe and sound. How are you doing today?" I smiled.

"Feeling blessed, ma'am." He returned the smile.

"Glad to hear. How's your head?"

"Still attached," he quipped. "Why do you ask?"

"Just wondered if it got injured in the explosion," I continued. One of the many sad things about war is the traumatic brain injury (TBI). We check every patient. It also helps to know if their brain is injured when we're communicating with the patient, because they can have difficulty understanding our instructions.

The LT and I talked for a while longer. Within a very few minutes I realized he was a sharp, positive, charming, charismatic young man, one of those people whom I would gladly assist any time. I went about my day with a warm fuzzy inside. When I returned to my office a couple of hours later, my staff had been receiving calls from some high-ranking officers in Washington, DC, inquiring about the LT. They wanted to make sure we were going to get him on the next flight. Actually they seemed kind of bossy about it. We give everyone quality care and for someone to tell me how to do my job . . . yes, I was offended. I am human. Plus the LT was so nice, how could we not bend over backwards helping him?!

Later that day I returned to the ICU and stopped in to see the LT. He was on Skype and he asked me to come around and say hi to his father. I half expected some gruff higher-ranking officer as I peeked around the screen. Instead I saw a soft-faced, concerned father, frightened for his child. And as I listened to their conversation and interactions, I began to sympathize with Colonel Lee. After an appropriate time I started to leave. The LT was telling his dad not to worry, that he had it under control.

I turned and smiled. "Cut your dad some slack LT. His son just got hurt." I winked.

"Yes ma'am," was the crisp reply.

One patient advocate once told me that there are three sides to every story. You just have to hear the other person's point of view. I still find it amusing that in the same day, I went from being frustrated with some seemingly overbearing colonel to being sympathetic with a fellow parent.

⌒⌒

The medevac flight brought in several wounded to the emergency room early that morning. As the more critical patients were triaged through and trundled off to the operating room, I was left behind with delayed and minimal wounded. Some were sent off for laboratory studies and others sent to radiology while I began working through the soldiers sitting on the bench. Along the way I met Jack Potts.

"What a great name!" I smiled.

"I like it. My dad and my granddad share the name too."

"What brings you to my ER?" I asked. That question allowed him the opportunity to talk, to narrate the events that led to his fractured leg. Jack required large amounts of morphine to get pain relief, but that only lasted a very short time. I checked the splint, the foot, the skin, everything I could think of, and then asked if he had received any valium or muscle relaxant.

"Oh no, ma'am." He seemed alarmed. "I don't need valium."

After the patients arrived on the medevac flight, they were rushed to the field hospital and quickly triaged. MARINE CORPS PHOTO

"But you are using morphine," I countered.

"That's for pain. Valium is for anxiety. I'm not panicky. I'm just in pain."

"Valium is a muscle relaxant. The muscle is attached to the tibia and your tibia is in three different pieces. A muscle relaxant would help. Can you trust me on this one?"

A puzzled expression passed his face and then he nodded, "I can take an order, ma'am. I'm a good Marine."

"All right, then. It's this doctor's order for you to try one dose of valium." And so Jack took one dose of valium.

Fifteen minutes later, I walked past his cot and he caught my eye. "Any better, Jack?" I asked.

"You were right, ma'am."

I couldn't hide my smile.

—Lt. Col. Gail Fancher

Sometimes obstacles and setbacks require course corrections that lead to crossroads in life. Some fear making a choice and never move on; others discover a path they never knew existed. . . .

"I Have the best job in the World"

When I was in high school, a friend of my sister was a single-engine pilot. For my sixteenth birthday, her gift to me was a flight with her friend. I instantly fell in love with flying and knew I wanted to fly for a living. I took lessons, and when I turned eighteen I got my private pilot's license. While I was taking lessons I did some research and found that the Air Force would provide me the best opportunities to fly and have a career in aviation. I also found that if I had the grades and got letters of recommendation from teachers and congressmen, I might have a chance at the Air Force Academy, and fulfill my dream to become a pilot. I was willing to fly anything, from cargo planes to fighter jets. Just get me up there in the wild blue. That was my goal and what I wanted to do as a career. Then life happened, things changed, and I never went to the Academy. Specifically, I ended up getting married, that marriage ended in divorce, and I never followed that dream. When I was twenty-eight years old I had open heart surgery. I had a congenital defect, which needed to be repaired or else I would have died of a heart attack by the time I was in my forties. I had the surgery, and it was then I decided I wanted to be a cardiac nurse. I went to nursing school at Auburn University in Alabama, and accomplished what I set out to do. I worked in a cardiac ICU and became a cardiac nurse.

After a few years working in the cardiac ICU, I moved and worked in the cath lab and became the senior electrophysiology nurse. This job was hard and we worked long hours, but I loved every minute of it. We had to cover emergency calls a few nights a week and on the weekends, and it was one night on call when I met the chief nurse at the 908th Aeromedical Staging Squadron at Maxwell Air Force Base. My team got paged around one in the morning to come in to the cath lab for a gentleman who was having a heart attack.

We got there, did the procedure on him, and saved his life. After the procedure I went to speak to his wife to let her know her husband was doing well and she could see him soon. We then got to talking, and that is how my military career began.

My patient happened to be the chaplain at Maxwell AFB, and his wife was the chief nurse at the 908th. I sat and spoke with her for a while about her husband's procedure and visited with her several times during his hospital stay. We got to talking about the military, and that is when I found out they were both in. She talked to me about critical care air transport teams (CCATT), and I immediately wanted to do it.

She described CCATT as a flying ICU. It is a three-person team composed of one critical care physician, one critical care nurse, and a critical care respiratory therapist. They are equipped with 750 pounds of equipment and can transport up to six critically wounded warriors, with three being on ventilators, on any mode of transport the Air Force had (aircraft, Humvees, ambulances, etc.). CCATT had been established in the Air Force since 1996 and the 908th had one CCAT team on their manning document but did not have the personnel to fill the slots.

After 9/11 my desire to join the military had increased again, and this seemed like the perfect time to finally pursue that dream. I told her I was interested, but I thought I was too old to join the military. It turned out I was not, and I immediately contacted a recruiter. I told him I had already spoken to the chief nurse at the 908th about how she wanted me as her CCATT nurse, and that I wanted to sign on the dotted line. This was in 2002.

When I learned I needed open heart surgery, I realized life was too short, that people were precious and time was not guaranteed. I needed to do something important and becoming a nurse and saving lives, like someone did for me, seemed like the right thing to do. As stated earlier, my initial goal in life was to become a pilot, but I now believe things happen for a reason. Becoming a cardiac nurse and saving the chaplain's life that night put me on the path to my military career. Not only could I be a nurse, but I could be a nurse for the best country in the world and take care of true heroes.

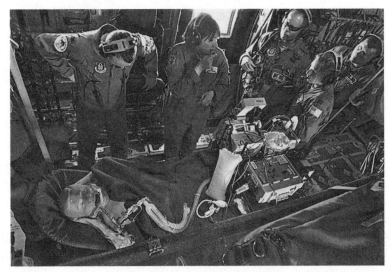

Training is vital for the doctors and nurses of CCATT to maintain a high level of proficiency as they care for critically wounded servicemen and women. AIR FORCE PHOTO

Because of my open heart surgery, it took almost a year for the surgeon general to approve me to join the military. They required several pieces of documentation from my cardiologist saying that I was fit for duty. Finally, on March 31, 2003, I raised my right hand and joined the US Air Force Reserves.

I started drilling at the unit. I went to Reserve Commissioned Officer Training School for four weeks at Maxwell in 2003 and started my CCATT training in 2004, and I have been with them ever since. If it wasn't for being on call that night for the Cath lab, and saving the chaplain's life, I would not be in the military doing the job I love so much. They say people meet for a reason and there was definitely a reason for me being on call that night and meeting them.

Over the past ten years I have flown over a hundred CCATT missions and have transported more than a hundred wounded warriors. In Iraq, the base was constantly getting bombed, but we never thought about it. We were there to do a mission, and it was our job to get the wounded troops home to their loved ones.

Some missions were harder than others, each one had a different story, but all tugged at our heart strings. Every single time I walked into the ICU to package our patients for the flight, my breath was immediately taken away and I got teary-eyed. Seeing the young men and women, lying in their beds with blast injuries that can only happen in a war zone, definitely makes you have a new perspective on life. What these boys and girls were willing to do to protect our freedom is beyond remarkable.

I will never forget one mission we did. We had to fly further down-range, to Tallil, Iraq, to pick up a nineteen-year-old boy who had lost both of his legs in an IED blast. When we walked into the ICU, I immediately had a connection with him. To this day I still can't figure out what it was, but I never left his side for twenty-four hours. We picked him up, brought him to Balad for more definitive care, and my team volunteered to take him to Germany (where Landstuhl Military Hospital is) because he requested that I remain his nurse.

When we got on the back of the aircraft in Tallil, and it was time to take off, I was unable to leave his side. Every time I tried to walk away to

As the transport plane ascended above the clouds, it came under attack from surface-to-air missiles, and had to dispatch counter-measures to keep from getting hit. AIR FORCE PHOTO

get to my seat for takeoff he would raise his head and grab my hands. The pilots of the aircraft were getting impatient because we needed to take off, but I refused to leave my patient's side. So the aeromedical evacuation crew strapped me to the side of his litter so I would not be tossed around during the combat takeoff we had to perform.

During takeoff the aircraft started to get shot at by surface-to-air missiles. Needless to say it was a rough ride out of the airport, but no matter what, no matter how scared we all felt, I continued to hold my patient's hand. Once at altitude I was able to free myself from the litter, but I continued to stand by his side, hold his hand, and talk to him. I assumed he knew he lost his legs, but I soon found out he didn't know.

At some point during the flight back to Balad, he looked up at me and asked me if he had in fact lost both of his legs. I immediately started to tear up knowing that I had to be the one to tell this nineteen-year-old that yes, he did lose both of his legs. He acknowledged what I told him and reached out his arms, put them around me, hugged me, patted me on the back and told me not to worry, that he was going to be okay! I will never forget that young man and that mission as long as I live.

He was just one of the stories I have tucked away in my memory. Each mission and each patient had a story, whether it was a personal story, a devastating injury, a family member waiting to greet them when we brought them home, or the camaraderie and teamwork displayed by the medical evacuation crews and aircraft crews on the back of the plane. Being CCATT and transporting our wounded warriors home is definitely the best job in the world. I also believe it is a selfish job for me. I get to wear the uniform of a country I love, and get true heroes home to receive more definitive care and treatment or keep them alive long enough for their family and loved ones to be able to say their final goodbyes.

And every day, I always think if it wasn't for being a part of the team that saved the life of the chaplain for Maxwell AFB, I would not be doing the best job in the world, which is caring for America's heroes!!

—Trish Hayden, Air Force Critical Care Air Transport (CCATT) Nurse

AFGHANISTAN

Every generation of Americans has a landmark event that defines their future for years to come. For those who endured the devastation of the Great Depression, they soon became "the Greatest Generation," after the Japanese attack on Pearl Harbor, which plunged the United States into World War II.

Sixty years later, on September 11, 2001, terrorists seized four American passenger planes and attacked New York's World Trade Center and The Pentagon in Washington, DC. The fourth plane failed to hit its target—believed to be another vital DC building, the Capitol or possibly even the White House—and plunged into a farm field in Pennsylvania, killing all aboard. Several thousand Americans were killed and wounded in these attacks, but the entire country was devastated. It was immediately compared to the attack on Pearl Harbor.

Soon after, it was learned that the terrorists had been trained in Afghanistan, and the Pentagon was ordered to formulate plans to dispatch combat units there, to take the fight to those who dared to attack America. Over the next two decades, thousands of American servicemen and women joined Coalition forces at sprawling bases and remote outposts in Afghanistan, a desolate country of sweltering heat, bone-chilling winters, and impassable mountains.

For combat units, they were stretched to the max between deployments to both Iraq and Afghanistan, and the prolonged missions strained those involved, including their family members back home. While many casualties in Iraq occurred in cities such as Fallujah and Baghdad, or along major thoroughfares, in Afghanistan often firefights and ambushes occurred in remote areas such as isolated combat outposts, and perilous mountain ranges and valleys, too far away for a vehicle to transport the wounded to an aid station within the golden hour, and almost impossible for medevac helicopters to get to, not that they didn't try. More than anything, the transportation of battlefield casualties is what differentiates Afghanistan from Iraq. The devastating injuries from sniper bullets and roadside explosives are the same in both conflicts, but the timetable was radically, and tragically stacked against those combatants in The Stan.

There is a common belief within the medical community that if an injured patient is delivered to an emergency room within sixty minutes of their accident, they have a better chance of surviving. It's called the golden hour. In a war zone, under heavy fire, in crappy weather, at inaccessible locales, sometimes it's virtually impossible to send out a helicopter or an ambulance, scoop up the injured combatant, and make a mad dash to the nearest medical facility. Following is one of those instances when the injured soldier was a helpless bystander to his own demise, and despite everyone's best efforts, it wasn't enough. Time became his worst enemy.

An Exasperating Wait

After an exhausting day at our aid station at Shindand Air Base in western Afghanistan, I was asleep in my bed when the door flew open and a flight medic stood in the door. It was around one in the morning and I was in a little bit of a daze, but I noticed he was standing there in his flight suit with his helmet on. I noticed it had the outline of a skull on it.

"Come quick . . . there's been an explosion and we need you . . . now!"

While I got dressed he briefed me that a mission had departed at dusk to recover a broken down vehicle that had hit a mine. There were four soldiers inside and three were injured—one seriously—and we had to go get them.

I began to gather items into my aid bag as other medics and Dr. Randy Richter came by to assess the situation and ensure I had everything we needed. He was still in his underwear and he gave me a quick pep talk: "Jerome, do your best. You know what you are doing so don't worry about being scared. You'll do great out there. May God be with you." It was exactly what I needed to hear to focus on my mission.

I ran out of the aid station and jumped into a waiting vehicle that sped off to the Black Hawk helicopter already going through pre-flight and preparing to leave. We all strapped in and the Black Hawk spun up and we took off. But rather than heading off to the crash site, we repositioned and awaited flight launch approval.

After what seemed like forever, we finally got the green light, lifted off, and flew over the base and out into the darkness. As we approached the site of the mine strike, we could see the front tires of the Humvee were ablaze, like a beacon in the dark night. We circled a couple of times and then lifted up again. I knew there were injured soldiers down there

"After what seemed like forever, we finally got the green light, lifted off, and flew over the base and out into the darkness."
AIR FORCE PHOTO

and asked what the issue was. The pilot came on and let me know there were additional mines visible to the female lieutenant who was in the disabled vehicle. As such, it was a hot LZ and it was just too risky to touch down. We hovered for approximately ten minutes trying to figure out what to do. When there's injured involved, even one minute can make a difference between life and death. I sat in the back, helpless, frustrated . . . defeated, knowing we had to get down there.

I thought through the variables and assessed the situation, and then I said something that even surprised me . . . I asked the pilot to get permission to hover a few feet off the ground and let me jump to the hood of the vehicle. We were wasting precious time just hovering high above the accident site, and now one of the casualties had become unconscious and was having a hard time breathing. I was Airborne qualified and jumping from the helicopter to the hood of the vehicle was little more than a bunny hop.

It seemed like a good solution to our current dilemma. Luckily, the LT onsite was a former enlisted medic and was doing her best to keep the soldier alive as we attempted to figure out a way to get down to them. The pilot seemed shocked and asked me to repeat what I had just said, so I did, this time with more conviction and urgency. He took a deep breath and sent the request up to the tactical operations center (TOC), which sent the request up to Bagram where the Country Headquarters and senior military leadership was located. After a few minutes of deliberation, I was informed that the request had been denied due to concern that the rotator wash from the helicopter could detonate the mines. Reluctantly we returned to the base

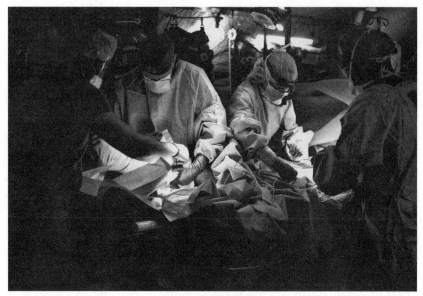

"I . . . yelled for my medics to get outside and start triage. Controlled chaos.
Mass casualty situation. Medics performed brilliantly. . . ." MARINE CORPS PHOTO

and I proceeded to the aid station, frustrated and feeling like I'd failed our
soldiers who depended on us to care for them.

It was now dawn and the sun was peeking over the distant mountains as we landed at our base. I headed up to the battalion TOC to find
out what was going on. The decision had been made to send out another
helicopter from Kandahar, this one with Navy para-rescue, to be lowered
to the vehicle and recover the injured soldiers. It would take over an hour
for the new crew to reach them. I returned to the aid station and briefed
everyone to be ready to receive the patients. As we reviewed how triage
and treatment would proceed, a runner from the TOC arrived stating that
a civilian van had driven by the vehicle and struck one of those exposed
mines in the roadway.

The next hour was tediously slow as we prepared for patients of
unknown number and injury from the US military vehicle and now from
the civilian van that were both inbound to us for treatment. We waited
and listened for an approaching helicopter and watched the horizon for
a speeding vehicle kicking up a trail of dust, but there was nothing, and

eventually we wondered if some other glitch was delaying us from doing our job.

Eventually a company commander entered the aid station and asked for her medics to come back to the unit and help with inventories in preparation for their unit departing the country, at least until and if they were actually needed. We walked outside together just as a van pulled up in front of our aid station. It was filled with multiple civilians with horrific injuries. The door opened and a leg fell out that was obviously from a young patient. The company commander almost fainted right there. I turned back and threw open the door to the aid station and yelled for my medics to get outside and start triage. We instantly moved into action.

It was a drill we had done dozens of times before with patients, but not with this many. It was controlled chaos. There were eight total, three of them with amputations or near amputations. One unconscious. One with severe head trauma. One had trouble breathing and two were covered in blood with multiple lacerations. It was a mass casualty situation and the entire base mobilized to assist us.

Despite the enormity of the carnage, the medics performed brilliantly. Patients were unloaded and triaged. I moved into the aid station to begin rendering aid. Dr. Richter, a Special Forces medic, and I each worked on the worst patients while the other medics monitored the others and assisted us as needed. The battalion commander and command sergeant major showed up and asked what we needed.

We immediately put out the call for combat lifesavers, who have received more than just basic first-aid training and could assist with the treatment. As they arrived, we continued to stabilize the worst patients and prepped them for evacuation. Despite the chaos and the carnage, our medical team was amazing.

We placed tourniquets, performed emergency cricothyrotomies, inserted chest tubes, began administering fluids, and stabilized patients. I can truly say that on that day we worked as a well-oiled machine in treating these Afghan civilians. Treatment continued for the critical patients and the medics and combat lifesavers focused their efforts on stabilizing the other patients' wounds.

We had sent out a medevac request for the patients when unexpectedly the Navy helicopters arrived with the wounded soldiers from the vehicle destroyed by the mine. We had been so absorbed with the civilians and the enormity of their injuries that we had not tracked the extraction or the status of those soldiers.

They unloaded the new patients and brought them into the aid station. Dr. Richter and I worked on the two conscious patients and stabilized them. We performed trauma surveys and prepped them for evacuation to the combat support hospital. We had been informed on the flight line that one of the soldiers had passed away. He was brought in and placed in our private area that we used for treatment that required private evaluations or disrobing. He was in a black body bag. Dr. Richter went in first and began the process of declaration as I completed the paperwork on the new patients. He unzipped the bag and did the initial survey of the soldier. I came in as he finished and he said, "Make sure I am not wrong, please." I immediately reacted and placed my finger on the deceased soldier's neck looking for a pulse and my stethoscope on his chest listening for breath and heart sounds. I was still focused on taking care of patients and was operating in complete reaction mode.

For declaration, there had to be five minutes of no breath or heart sounds. At this time, I was alone with him and was performing the examination as Dr. Richter organized the litter teams. As I waited for the time to elapse, I looked at the young soldier's face. His eyes were closed and there was no blood or dirt on his face. He looked so peaceful. I didn't know him. He had arrived just a few days before and was simply doing his job. As I learned later, he was the "go-to" guy for everything. He was a mechanic and had taken the place of an MP to ensure that the recovery went without any problems. It was not his mission, but he volunteered to go to take care of the soldiers and the vehicle. His eyes were closed and he simply looked asleep. I kept staring at him and felt the emotions of the day wash over me. My eyes teared up and rivers flowed down my cheeks. I really didn't care if anyone noticed. As the five minutes finished, I put my hand on his chest and closed my eyes. I was now very aware of what had happened that day and of the impact of what I had just done.

I whispered "I am so sorry I couldn't get out there. I tried." I said a little prayer and then rejoined the rest of the aid station crew as we began moving patients to the flight line for loading for movement to the field hospital for further treatment.

Usually we do not load live and deceased patients together, but we didn't have enough aircraft or space to wait. The next helicopter

Their mission is to get to the site and transport the wounded within that crucial golden hour, but all too often that becomes an impossible goal. ARMY PHOTO

would not be available for at least an hour, so we chose to load them all on the aircraft waiting to take off. There was confusion and emotions on the flight line, but Dr. Richter spoke up and said, "Let's get him home."

Without hesitation we prepped the body and loaded him on a stretcher. We moved the soldier's body to the aircraft as the last to load and placed him in the helicopter with the Navy para-rescue that had just extracted him. It was a blur and things were happening so fast.

It was just muscle memory of what we had done so many times before. However, after we finished and moved out from beneath the spinning rotators, our Special Forces medic turned and snapped to attention and rendered a salute. His experiences from losing a team member just a couple of months before had guided him to this action. We all followed suit and stood there as they lifted off for the hour and a half journey to the field hospital. We had no time to take it in as we still had patients that needed assistance.

We ran off to the aid station and continued treatment on the remaining patients and the newly arriving patients from the mine explosion. The local village was still collecting more wounded and sending them to us to take care of them. None of the new patients were that badly injured, but they did inform us of a couple of people who had been killed. It only added to the emotional weight of the day.

Colonel Richter and Major Wenninger worked together at the aid station at Shindand Air Base in western Afghanistan. JEROME WENNINGER'S PERSONAL PHOTO

We completed the work of evaluation, stabilization, treatment, and stitching, and once it all quieted down we rotated people for dinner as it was nightfall. After we finished, we had to get busy on cleaning up and resetting the aid station for anything that might happen next. After one hell of a day, it was difficult to focus, but it was necessary as our mission had not changed and soldiers were still out working at the scene with antitank mines littering their area. Late that night, we all huddled and did an after-action review (AAR) of the day's events.

One by one, we reviewed the course of events and gave our evaluation of our actions and what we could have done better. Medics who had arrived just hours before to this location had seen the worst of war and were forced to face their emotions and performance in a very difficult way on this day. We allowed our emotions to flow and as needed, we were there for one another. It was our own way of coping with the emotional demands of the day.

It had been a very long and hard day for all of us, and we went to bed knowing that we would never be the same. We felt good about what we had done, but also had a new sense of mortality about our mission. It is a day that I often replay in my head. I was fortunate enough to have great medics, great leaders, and support on that day. I am still friends with Dr. Richter to this day, and he is a trusted mentor. Throughout my medical career I have often turned to him for help and advice. We speak often, but we have never talked about that day. I do still talk to the Special Forces medic. He continues to serve and has been an incredible military medical provider.

I was able to meet the battalion commander, Colonel Hayes, six years later in Korea for dinner. As we caught up and talked about the time that had passed, he stopped me and asked: "For six years I have wondered, if I had let you jump from the helicopter, would you have been able to save him?" I knew who he was talking about. As I found out later, the soldier who had passed had sustained a horrible close head injury that caused his brain to swell and there would have been nothing I could have done to save him, even if I had gotten to him when we flew out to the crash site. I looked directly at the colonel, knowing his pain, and simply said, "No sir, there was nothing I could have done that night to save him." He dipped his head and took a deep breath and simply said, "Thank you." He had been second-guessing his decision for six years, and I finally relieved his pain. Still, neither one of us can ever forget that brave soldier.

My father was an Army Ranger in Vietnam. I never would have known if it wasn't for my mother. Years after this hellish night in Afghanistan, I sat down with him and we talked about combat for the first time ever. He told me about his friend who had been shot, and he had carried him for miles to an aid station, not knowing his friend had died from his injuries. When I told him about my experience, he couldn't understand the weight of it. It was beyond what he could comprehend, even with everything he had seen and experienced in Vietnam. We talked about it and helped one another. It was the one and only time my father and I have ever talked about our experiences in combat, and the one time we understood the heavy burden people go through during those times, and sometimes for years after.

We shared things in a way that helped us both to

"My father . . . an Army Ranger . . . carried him for miles to an aid station, but his buddy died before he could get there."
STARS AND STRIPES PHOTO

understand one another in a way we never had before. Since then I've treated hundreds of patients, many of them critical, but this one soldier I couldn't get to on that mine-laden road in Afghanistan is the one I can't forget. He is "The One" who fuels me and keeps me striving to be the best provider that I can. He will never be forgotten, and regardless of what I could have done, I still wish I could have been there for him that dark, cold night in Afghanistan. Maybe I could have made a difference.

—Jerome Wenninger, Physician Assistant, US Army

Local nationals and laborers working with the US military often come from poor families. Sometimes, their close proximity to American combatants affords them an opportunity to improve their situation, whether it's eating better than they've ever done . . . or absconding with something they shouldn't.

For reasons of host nation sensitivities, the following story occurred in "Shangri-La," that fictitious country made famous in April of 1942, when President Franklin D. Roosevelt was asked where the Doolittle Raiders had taken off from. And because the author is still deployed downrange in Shangri-La, he is known but to a few close associates as Dr. Strike.

Petty Thievery in Shangri-La

We had a local national soldier come into my aid station for treatment of some superfluous condition, complaining of foot ailments, but we suspected he was either malingering or simply wanted medication he could later sell on the black market. Maybe he thought he could just complain about foot problems and we'd dole out whatever drugs he really wanted, but of course we had to examine his feet and immediately found that he was wearing my boots, which had gone missing from the front of my hooch where I had been drying them after a recent mission. I guess he failed to notice my name written inside.

Of course with the language issues he could feign ignorance, pretending not to understand what we were asking him about, but when we showed him my name inside the boot, and pointed from me to the boots, he clearly knew he'd been caught red-handed. He certainly understood enough English to recognize we were contacting his supervisor, because he rapidly disappeared from the aid station.

A little while later he returned to the aid station, carrying my boots, and demanded that he talk to me through some other soldier who did a half-assed job of interpreting for him. But my medic informed him he wasn't going to be demanding anything of anyone, so then the thief promptly threw my boots at my medic. We reported all this through his chain of command and I heard later that someone kicked the crap out of him, not because he'd stolen from the US forces trying to rebuild his country, but because he'd been foolish enough to get caught doing it!

I wish I could say this was an isolated case of petty thievery, but we knew it was part of an almost daily pattern of misdeeds. It was very well known the local soldiers smoked pot in the fields, often pulled weapons on our guys over minor disagreements, had accidental discharges of their weapons at inopportune times—when is there ever an opportune time?—and generally hindered and endangered the missions. Granted there were a very few outstanding local national soldiers, NCOs, and officers, but the norm was the opposite. To say this country was literally a den of thieves would be a vast understatement.

—"Dr. Strike" in Shangri-La

An early morning run is a great way to jump start the battery, get the juices flowing, clear the mind, and think about what needs to be done that day. Even in a war zone, it is possible to work out, though often it is accompanied by gunfire off in the distance, swirling dust kicked up by inbound helicopters, or passing battle wagons on their way to confront the enemy beyond the perimeter fence. For Robert Strange, his morning run came at the end of a very long night . . . a night he'll never be able to let go of.

Run to Forget

As I approached the guard station at the inner wire of our compound, I thought back to my cultural awareness courses at Fort Lewis. The protocols cover the basics . . . always remove your sunglasses when speaking with the Afghani people, place your hand over your heart as if you are back in grade school starting the day, reciting the Pledge of Allegiance, etc. The appropriate phrase to use as I approached the guard station was "Assalaam alaikum."

This phrase is spoken throughout the Muslim world and literally means "Peace be upon you." Unfortunately, the Afghanis speak thirty-two languages and dialects. Dari (a form of Farsi) is spoken most widely and is used by the government in Kabul. But even Dari has several dialects, and most people are fairly distrustful of the government in Kabul. In fact the name Afghanistan refers to "the land of the allied tribes." Trouble is, the tribes aren't so "allied." Fortunately, I am told by our interpreters that work with us that my "Assalaam alaikum" is accurate enough as to not cause any confusion for my Afghani listener.

The ANP (Afghan National Police) guard at the gate smiles and waves me through. I laugh to myself, knowing that he had recently confided to one of my colleagues that his AK-47 is "old and doesn't work well." But he and his counterparts are there with their malfunctioning AK-47s guarding the ramparts of our compound. Not very reassuring. I walk up to our "track," which really isn't much of a track, just a path of packed dirt camouflaged by the surrounding desert terrain.

Nevertheless, as the wind from the northwest picks up, a small cloud of dust emerges and will shower the track with fine unpacked dirt again. The track runs parallel to the runway at a safe enough distance that planes can take off and land without either party feeling concerned that

The Afghan National Police guard at the main gate, tasked with protecting the Americans stationed there from insurgent attacks, had a malfunctioning weapon and wasn't too concerned about it. ARMY PHOTO

a collision between the two will occur. The sun warms my skin, which hasn't seen sunlight in the last twenty-four hours. The season has turned the temperature today to a very comfortable 32 degrees Celsius (89.6 Fahrenheit). This comfort comes from both the lack of humidity and my body having finally acclimated to my surroundings.

I keep my head up as I run. While I don't have to worry about the planes, I do need to look out for military vehicles sharing this path—just as one would be careful while walking in the rain in a busy city, because any minute a car might come upon a large puddle of water, showering the pedestrians on the sidewalk. A vehicle that gets too close to me will spray me with a cloud of dust. It is by no means an act of malice, just the result of the basic laws of nature regarding any moving object traveling in this land. I usually try to hold my breath if the cloud is a small one.

If it is too big, I can only force my lips closed and breathe through my nose and hopefully, my nose will filter some of the air before it hits the back of my throat on the way down to my lungs. Once in the lungs it burns and can only be relieved with a coughing fit—not compatible with keeping my run going. Today, I run to forget.

There's a sense of boredom we have all been experiencing this past week. It can lull all of us into a false sense of security of having little contact with the violence that sometimes occurs outside our gates. These were the feelings my team and I had been experiencing that week as we went to bed. I fell asleep without a problem as I usually do, but at some point that night the knocking on my door began. I hoped it was someone else's door, maybe the field workers from the "OGA" (other government agency we aren't supposed to name) across the hall or the helicopter crew from the dust-off unit down the hall. Those medevac guys get called out at all hours, day and night. But this time it was my door, and after the third round of knocking I had no choice but to get up and answer the call.

"Robbie, we have a twelve-year-old coming in, blown-up by an IED." The senior surgeon in my group speaks in an accent I am still not sure of, nor can I quite figure out where he is from. But he calls me Robbie and I don't mind it. I consider it a friendly nickname that reminds me of my family and a time of youthful innocence. Sometimes it seems so long ago.

I put in my contacts even though I don't need to. I brought no less than four pairs of glasses—all made by the military with bulletproof lenses. My surgical loupes have an insert with my prescription should I decide not to wear my contacts, which are the most comfortable items I put on in the morning. They are two little sponges of cool water (contact lens solution actually, but how do my eyes know the difference) that bathe my tired eyes still trying to adjust to the uninvited light.

I finish dressing with a pair of Navy exercise shorts, made with a lining that actually wicks away moisture from my skin, allowing me to continue my workout, or in this case perform surgical duties, hours on end without feeling the need to change. My tan T-shirt is made of the same material but lacks the identifying markings that my shorts have. Appropriately, my shorts are marked "NAVY" in all block reflective letters. Our official PT T-shirt is made of the same material as well, and boasts the same markings on the front and back but is the most hideous shade of yellow. Most are embarrassed to wear it. We only have two choices, the PT uniform or the Army camouflage uniform, ACUs.

Our choice to ignore the yellow shirt reminds me of Hawkeye Pierce and B. J. Hunnicutt from M*A*S*H and their failure to button their blouses revealing the all drab green army T-shirt—those rebels! Finally, I put on my tan Crocs. Not the Crocs our kids wear, but operating room Crocs. It's the same rubber material but lacks holes on the top for the obvious reason: to keep the "table scraps" from falling directly onto my feet. The shoes are vented on the side to provide the circulation necessary when one wears rubber shoes.

The Forney Clinic trauma bay has four beds, which are empty when I arrive. Only a few of the team has stumbled in, successfully emerging from their evening slumbers. The senior surgeon is still listed as being on-call, so I decide to take the head of the bed. I put on my trauma boots; these are blue, impervious covers that go over my shoes and reach just below my knees. I put on my black latex gloves and reach for the Littman II stethoscope. I prefer my own, but it didn't make the trip to Afghanistan.

I remind the corpsman at our table where to place the leads for the monitor to avoid interfering with obtaining a good x-ray. I hate missing shrapnel from an IED because it's obscured on the film by a radio-opaque lead. I ask who is manning the blood bank and remind him to wait for my command. Some in the room know the most important bit of information about the patient soon to arrive. Unfortunately, this fact has not been relayed to me yet.

Finally, the patient arrives accompanied by the Afghani surgeon who initially treated him at the hospital in Farah. I have probably performed thousands of these trauma resuscitations. Over and over, primary survey, secondary survey, taking care to immediately treat any of the six life-threatening conditions that if missed will take your patient's life in front of your eyes in the trauma bay.

Repetition, repetition, repetition allows this to become a reflex, like a hammer striking the knee, instead of the academic exercise it often is for the novice. Our patient is lethargic and having trouble with his airway. His respiratory effort is weak and a clear silicone tube is slid into his mouth, down his throat, through his vocal cords, and into his trachea. All of this is aided with the light from a laryngoscope, which also forces the tongue out of the way. The cuff at the end of the tube is inflated to

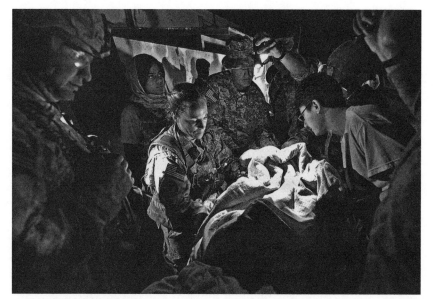

"The patient is only twelve years old . . . and near death. His body has been so starved of oxygen and is so cold that all of his normal reactions are either slowing or stopping altogether. He is headed for the multisystem organ failure that follows hemorrhagic shock if it is not addressed in the first hour, the golden hour of trauma." AIR FORCE PHOTO

prevent blood and secretions from slipping past his cords and around the tube into his lungs.

His chest now rises as we squeeze air out of the ambu-bag down through the endotracheal tube. But only the right side of his chest rises and falls with each breath. The patient is only twelve years old—we think; apparently no one knows their own age in Afghanistan (birthdays are not celebrated in this part of the world). His trachea is shorter in length than the typical adult. We have placed the tube down past his carina into his right main stem bronchus, thereby failing to allow air to pass into his left lung as well. We deflate the balloon and slide the tube back a few centimeters.

After the balloon is reinflated, both sides of the chest rise and fall. His trachea is in the midline; had it been deviated to one side we would be concerned about a collapsed lung under tension. Breath sounds are clear on both sides, further evidence of the lack of a collapsed lung or blood in the space around the lung. We have passed steps A and the B of the ABCDE of the primary survey. (It is a checklist that must be followed in order and no detail missed, whether it's at 2:00 p.m. or two in the morning.) The blood pressure cuff is going up, ECG leads are on, but not in the place I instructed and a few seconds are killed repositioning them. The rhythm is eerily normal sinus in the 70s.

The improvised explosive device, IED, blasted away a portion of the right side of his abdominal wall. Loops of his small bowel and a portion of his large bowel lay beside him (evisceration), and his right leg has nearly been amputated, but his heart rate is in the 70s. This is a terrible sign of something wrong.

A pulse is palpable in his neck but not in his groin or wrist. This means his blood pressure is approximately 60. The cuff finishes its cycle and reads 58/32—not bad for a physical exam correlation with a machine. But again something is wrong that his heart rate isn't much quicker.

We human beings are obligate aerobes—meaning we cannot exist without oxygen. Our blood acts like little boxcars, picking up a big load of oxygen at our lungs. Our heart is the big engine that pushes the boxcars around the tracks—our blood vessels—to deliver its precious cargo to the cells, billions and billions of greedy little cells that usually never have to wait for their regular and constant delivery of oxygen. After quickly unloading this oxygen, it is happily welcomed across the cell membrane into the energy factory of the cell—the mitochondria.

There are a series of reactions involving carbon derived from carbohydrates, fats, and proteins to produce the common energy currency in our cell—ATP. Should the regular supply of oxygen fail to arrive, the mitochondria will shift to a very inefficient process yielding much less ATP and worse—acid! This acid travels around the body and slows all the other reactions. But the body can combat this by keeping the supply of oxygen steady and on time. If some of the boxcars fall off the track (bleeding), the body can just pump the remaining boxcars faster—tachycardia (fast heart rate). But this kid's heart rate is only in the 70s. He is near death. His body has been so starved of oxygen and is so cold that all of his normal reactions are either slowing or stopping altogether. He is headed for

For the price of a meal for their entire family, any of these Afghan boys might be approached by the Taliban to dig a simple hole by a roadside and plant a cardboard box . . . loaded with explosives and a timer. ARMY PHOTO

the multisystem organ failure that follows hemorrhagic shock if it is not addressed in the first hour, the golden hour of trauma.

Soon I would learn the secret that many had been keeping from me. We roll back to the OR. We pour antiseptic solution on the patient and cover him with drapes. His abdomen is opened, the holes in his bowels and stomach quickly closed. The fecal material is removed from his peritoneal cavity, his abdomen covered with a special cloth I constructed out of Ioban, an antimicrobial plastic, and a simple blue OR towel. The edges of his abdomen are brought closer together, but not completely closed, with penetrating towel clips. We complete the amputation of his right thigh started by the IED blast. But it does not matter.

Three times and then a fourth time I massage his heart to bring back his blood pressure while the anesthesiologist infuses more adrenaline and acid buffering solution. More boxcars are infused as well as clotting protein solution (fresh frozen plasma). With each episode we restore signs of life back to this little twelve-year-old boy. But his fate has been sealed, sealed long before he ever arrived on our OR table.

"Their vehicle had struck an IED in an area previously cleared of IEDs . . . and again it starts over." *STARS AND STRIPES* PHOTO

It wasn't that he had actually been the one to bury the IED. How could we blame him? The boy and his family are poor and they need to eat like the rest of us to feed the little ATP machine in all of our cells. The Taliban will pay him enough money to feed his family for months. Back at our FOB (forward operating base) we can buy a daily supply of this wonderful flat bread for three weeks for only $5. The entire twenty-man staff is able to have a piece. The people that sell us the bread think they are ripping us off for $5. We think we are robbing from them. All this boy has to do is bury the IED, the Taliban will do the rest—easy money.

What would you do if your family was starving and foreigners were in your country? He didn't count on there being a problem with the wiring as he stood up to walk away. But this isn't the secret that they had been keeping from me . . . and then they tell me. The IED went off five hours ago. You see, we will treat all comers regardless of their age, sex, religion, nationality, criminal activity, etc. but we can't raise the dead. His fate had been sealed before he even arrived at our base, let alone to our OR table. It was written on the monitor; his temperature had never risen above 31 degrees C (88 F) despite blowing hot air on his skin and actively warming all of the fluids we infused. His acid level was so high and his organs had long ago started to shut down before he arrived. Each time I pumped his heart I knew it was futile, but now I was just treating myself and my teammates, many of us who are fathers with sons of our own. How could someone delay the treatment of their son? How could the hospital in Farah wait to transfer him? Had they been mad because he worked for the Taliban? Maybe they thought he would die any minute and when he didn't maybe they decided he might make it after all and needed to see the doctor. It's likely I'll never find out why they waited . . . there was

He was just a typical Afghan boy who spent his entire life in a war zone. His body was devastated by an improvised explosive device he planted on the roadside. He died from his injuries. ARMY PHOTO

nothing more we could do. After making sure all of his blood was off my skin, I crawled into bed. Surely we would get to sleep in; after all we never muster on Fridays. Three hours later the knocks started on my door again. This time I assembled my gear a little quicker.

The dust-off crew was off to bring us three more patients. This time they would be folks fighting along with our Special Forces—the ANA (Afghan National Army). Their vehicle had struck an IED in an area previously cleared of IEDs . . . and again it starts over.

ABCDE . . . finally, I get a break and now I am not running to get exercise or to work on the tan that has started to fade after lack of sunshine. Now, I am running, lips closed, breathing through my nostrils as the dust cloud passes over, I am running to forget . . . but how can I ever forget a little boy who never had a chance?

—Robert Strange

To everything there is a season, and a time to every purpose under the heaven.

—Ecclesiastes 3:1 (King James Bible version)

The Killing Season

T he Taliban on Wednesday announced the start of their Spring fighting season, just hours after President Obama concluded a surprise visit to Afghanistan," reported the *Washington Post* on May 2, 2012.

For my unit the "Fighting Season" had already begun since spring had come early that year, in early April, and by May we had already transported hundreds of American and NATO forces to the Role 3 treatment facility at Kandahar Airfield, situated in the RC-South region of Afghanistan. This medical unit, comparable to any trauma center in most US cities, included a twelve-bed emergency room, six surgical suites, a lab, a

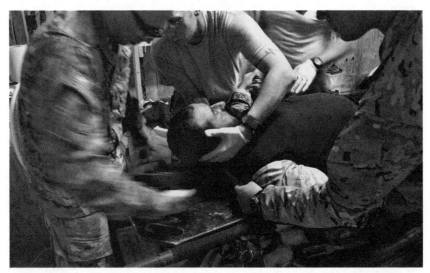

"The Role 3 facility at Kandahar Airfield . . . comparable to any trauma center in most US cities." The injuries though—from improvised explosive devices, sniper bullets, rocket attacks, and mortar barrages—were unique to a war zone such as Afghanistan. ARMY PHOTO

pediatric unit, and a psychology department, as well as dental, veterinary, and x-ray, CT, and MRI capabilities.

On that day in early May, I had just begun my mid-tour leave, and knew when I returned I would be there to burden the gauntlet of what the media called the Fighting Season. I call it the Killing Season, since it often brought the slaughter of the innocents who were killed for no reason other than to torment those of us who were there to protect them. Even though my leave was for twenty-one days, a third of it was eaten up just getting to and back from my home in Hawaii. My wife and I also went to Las Vegas for a couple of days after spending some much needed time resting at home. I tried not to think about what was going on with my crew while I was gone, but I did keep a keen eye on the news to ensure that there weren't any helicopter accidents while I was away.

I did know that once I got back downrange I would be going to Forward Operating Base (FOB) Pasab, which I knew would be the very worst of the war for me. Certainly I had my own doubts about heading back downrange, so I did everything I could so my wife had the time of her life with me, just in case I didn't make it back home alive. Once I got back in the saddle, it was time to refocus all my energy on the task at hand, which is providing life-saving care to our wounded brothers and

"It was my first time being the first up medic . . . which meant our crew would be the first one airborne. . . ." CHRISTOPHER WASHBURN PERSONAL PHOTO

sisters. We had established the Platinum Ten, in which our goal was to be in the air in ten minutes and onsite in ten minutes or less. Our unit established numerous sites within our Area of Responsibility, which was all of RC South. The media had already reported that we had two crews at Kandahar Airfield, initially three at Forward Operating Base Pasab (later a fourth crew was added), two at FOB Sikari Karez, three at

FOB Wolverine, three at FOB Tarin Kot, and two more at FOB Spin Boldak.

Pasab was our busiest, and the most missions we'd had during one week had been fourteen. The primary reason for these forward-based medevac teams was an incident that happened before we arrived in theater, when a soldier died due to the previous medevac unit not launching until an armed escort was ready. To alleviate that issue, we all knew and understood our mission was to save our wounded brothers and sisters, and so we launched every day and every time a call came in, even if we didn't have an armed escort helicopter to provide overwatch protection. Always, our goal was to be onsite in less than ten minutes.

Many times we flew into Siah Choy, an area within the Panjwai Valley I considered the most evil place in the world, since in one week's time myself and two other flight medic crews transported over one hundred American soldiers who were Category A patients, meaning they all had injuries consisting of amputations; gunshot wounds to the chest, abdomen, and head; as well as complex lung and tissue injuries. If this same period had happened even a couple of years before, we would have had a body count similar to what was seen during the height of the Vietnam War.

This particular week's rotation started on May 28 and already our three crews had transported twenty-three American wounded just from Pasab to Role 3 in Kandahar in three days. The 30th started very early for me, since it was my first time being the first up medic at Pasab, which meant our crew was in a standby role and we would be the first one airborne when a call came in.

At 0605 we heard "Medevac, medevac, medevac" over the radio and we all jumped up and raced to get dressed, get to our aircraft, load our weapons, take the point of injury and the MIST reports, and dash out to the aircraft and get in the air as fast as we could. MIST stands for Mechanism (the cause of the injury), Injury (such as gunshot, IED, etc.), Signs of life (conscious or unconscious, airway, pulse, and blood pressure), and Treatment (what the patient had already received such as meds, a tourniquet, an IV, etc.). As we hustled to the bird already getting revved up, we knew one of our brothers from Task Force Fury—made up of

"We knew one of our brothers from Task Force Fury—made up of elements from the 82nd Airborne and 2nd Infantry divisions—was out there in the vast beyond, hurting and waiting for our help." ARMY PHOTO

elements from the 82nd Airborne and 2nd Infantry divisions—was out there in the vast beyond, hurting and waiting for our help. The medevac was headed out to snatch a Cat Alpha as we called them, wounded by an IED strike, in an open field with enemy in the area. The insurgents had done their damage, but now time was our enemy, and every minute wasted was another minute the wounded soldier couldn't afford to lose.

We were in the air and on our way within nine minutes of the call, since we all knew that seconds count during that golden hour. My adrenaline was pumping so hard, I was shaky . . . we all knew that whatever the MIST report stated was usually only a little bit right, and greatly understated what was wrong with the patient 98 percent of the time. Often assessments are made under fire and communicated with a high sense of urgency, so they're not always accurate. All we got was just the cause of their injuries, because everything else was useless to have since I would have to reassess anyway, once we arrived onsite.

Within thirteen minutes of the initial call, we were on the ground, threw the crew chief's door open, and ran out into the field, not knowing or caring if it was clear or not of IEDs, to get to the injured warrior and carry him back to the bird, where it was a sitting duck, out in an open field. There were no armed escort helicopters after March of 2012, but we all accepted the fact that we could do a more efficient job and execute the mission without waiting for escort birds to get ready to launch for a mission.

We were our own escort, and I and many other flight medics knew all the risks, since every day we got daily Intel briefs of what was going on in our regions. We all disregarded our own safety for the care of the injured soldiers and Marines; we fulfilled the DUSTOFF motto daily: Dedicated Unhesitating Service To Our Fighting Forces. At our other FOBs there were dedicated gunship escorts, but in the Panjwai Valley we only had ourselves. Whenever we were launched on a mission, there were always Kiowas and Apaches somewhere in the area, mostly due to their support of the ground troops and their operations, so we would always ask them to keep an eye out for us, but they were never directly in support of us on missions.

Without an armed escort helicopter, the medics were exposed to insurgent snipers while on the ground, carrying the injured soldier back to their helicopter. MARINE CORPS PHOTO

Once airborne, we maintained communications with the troops at the destination site, our trauma unit, and our tactical operations center, constantly updating the severity of the patient using a coding system from simple transport back to a care unit to the most critical—in-flight surgery that could not wait until we returned to our treatment facility. We never used the patient's real name over the communications network because personal information could be overheard and get back to their relatives in the States, who obviously would not yet have been told via official channels that their loved one had been injured, so in this particular case my patient's name was "Citrus Heights." At 0619 we were airborne again, en route to Role 3 at Kandahar Airfield. My patient had received good care on the ground, just tourniquets, but they were crucial in saving his life. He had been on a foot patrol in the heart of a Taliban stronghold when an IED exploded, one powerful enough to destroy a vehicle. It literally had

"But as a medic it is not up to me to decide who lives and who dies. I just do my part of trying to make a difference and that is all I ever wanted: to make a difference." CHRISTOPHER WASHBURN PERSONAL PHOTO

torn him to pieces and he was missing both legs at the upper thigh, his left arm to the shoulder, and he had a mutilated right forearm and bicep.

Even with all the morphine I gave him, he was still able to yell, cry, and plead with me to just let him die. I was certainly aware that an overdose of morphine would end his pain permanently, but my responsibility as a medic was to guard life for him and his family. He was after all someone's son. I continually dressed and redressed his wounds, took his vitals, established IV lines, controlled his airway, and kept him alive until I handed him over to the Role 3 ER staff at Kandahar. We landed at 0630, a little more than ten minutes after picking him up. I began my report to the doctor and nursing staff and didn't even realize I was crying while giving the report . . . it was so traumatic to see him like that. He was struggling to die and yet it was me who was struggling, doing all I could to keep him alive. As far as I know he is still alive somewhere stateside. . . .

Certainly I still think about him, and wonder how I would feel if I was injured so severely. I think back on that day and his unimaginable pain or the challenges he faces on a daily basis. But as a medic it is not up to me to decide who lives and who dies. I just do my part of trying to make a difference and that is all I ever wanted: to make a difference. As time passes, I will revisit these days downrange and wonder how they will affect me. Hopefully my understanding of it all will get better as time passes. For now, I will continue to do the best I can, for as long as I can, for my brothers and sisters in arms.

—Christopher Ray Washburn, Combat Medic

Most front-line warriors are lucky. They might get dinged up a few times, but they're still among the living, with all appendages still functioning. Other combatants, like Army Lt. Brian Brennan, weren't so lucky, though he doesn't use his injuries as an excuse. Instead they serve as motivation to overcome and conquer.

"Two Someones?"

It was an ordinary day, at least as ordinary as a day ever gets in a combat zone. The war in Afghanistan was thick in the midst of the spring offensive. I'd been busy taking care of my soldiers at our aid station sick call that morning—all routine stuff—when my radio went off. We had a medevac call, one I was destined to remember for the rest of my life.

Most medevac calls follow the same pattern: the pilot in command, medic, and flight surgeon run to the tactical operations center (TOC) to gather location, weather, and medical information. In the meantime, the other pilot and the crew chief run for the helicopter and prepare it to launch. In the TOC, we got our first indication this would not be a routine mission. Almost all of the information we were given was bad.

A convoy had hit a massive improvised explosive device and there were five urgent surgical patients—the worst category—all in critical condition. And the weather was flat horrible. Winds were kicking up and a thunderstorm was sweeping over the mountains and across the valley floor. Helicopters and weather like that don't mix, but at the same time, we knew if we didn't launch, there were soldiers out there who would die.

The only positive piece of information we were given was the location, a mere seven-minute flight across the valley floor with none of our usual treacherous mountain passes to navigate. Things were tense as the command group weighed our options, none of which were optimal. Launch now and risk the weather killing the ten aviation personnel on two aircraft. Or wait for the storm to pass and, in all likelihood, have no one left to save. On medevac, we understand the importance of the golden hour, and always want to launch even if the situation is bad. Being told no is an awful, helpless feeling. After a few minutes, we got launch approval, though it seemed like an eternity.

The weather was flat horrible, winds kicking up and thunderstorms, but if we didn't take off, there were wounded soldiers out there who would die.
AIR FORCE PHOTO

Running from the TOC to the aircraft, my mind was swirling, but was interrupted by another radio call. The patient load had been changed from five urgent surgical down to two urgent surgical and three KIA. If my focus could have become more intense, with that news, it did. With three KIA, that meant that the two surviving soldiers must be severely wounded. They would need everything we had and they would need it now.

I was still strapping on my gear as we lifted off: body armor, life support vest, helmet, gloves. I looked across our Black Hawk at our medic. Always intense, he was staring out the window and focused on the mission. We would be a team on this one. Then I glanced to the right at the crew chief. His facial expression mirrored the medic's.

Finally, I glanced back at our sister ship, a heavily armed Black Hawk with two 240mm guns mounted in the windows. That aircraft was our protection if this turned into an ambush. They had an additional flight medic on board in case there were more injuries than we were expecting. Or in case we became casualties.

As we flew, I soon learned what 40-knot wind gusts feel like. The aircraft was being blown around in the sky. Both the medic and the crew chief were silent, allowing the pilots to focus on flying. As we approached the site, we saw what was left of the vehicle in pieces scattered around a wide area and a large hole in the road, smoke billowing from the burning fuel. All I could think was "Wow, someone survived that? Two someones?"

We came in for a landing and the medic and I ran to the patients. I remember seeing the KIAs to my left ready for loading into our sister ship. The flight medic from our escort ship was already assessing one of the survivors, so we ran to the second one. I dimly registered him as a young lieutenant and a pretty big guy. Two tourniquets in place on each leg, both legs mangled from the knees down—just mush, though the bleeding was controlled. Left arm badly broken with another tourniquet. Good chest rise and fall. Clear airway. And no response at all.

The Glasgow Coma Scale rates the level of unconsciousness of a patient from a normal of 15 down to 3 being the lowest score possible: the same score that would be given to a fence post. He was a 3. Judging the flight time, the weather, and the severity of both soldiers' injuries, I decided to skip a step in our protocol and not place an endotracheal tube to help him breathe. He needed surgery, and he needed it now.

En route back, the medic and I worked silently on the two critically wounded men, communicating only with hand signals, while the pilots and helicopter battled the weather. I remember getting airborne in the back of the helicopter numerous times and crashing back down onto my knees, trying to hold on with one hand and do patient care with the other as the aircraft bucked the wind.

I wish I could say that I was smart enough to be scared, but I wasn't. At that moment, I was too focused. Scared would have to wait until later, when I had time to reflect.

We touched down and ran for the hospital. Within thirty seconds of arriving in the emergency

Due to bad weather, the helicopter was being buffeted, and all the while we worked to stabilize two critically wounded soldiers. DOD PHOTO

medical treatment area, the lieutenant went into cardiac arrest from blood loss. I was never so glad to have skipped a step in the protocol—had we followed it, he would not have survived. The surgeons put in massive IV lines and started pumping blood into him as fast as the pressure infusers would go, the entire combat support hospital team working in complete synchrony.

As I stood on the periphery, no longer engaged in actual care, I marveled at the seamless functioning of the team: surgeons, nurses, medics, lab, pharmacy, radiology, and so many more. Everyone had a task and everyone performed their task flawlessly. In less time than I would have imagined possible, he was rushed into the operating room where both legs were amputated and his arm was set, and other injuries efficiently stabilized. He was then moved to the ICU, still completely unresponsive and in extremely critical condition, death only a heartbeat away.

It was at this point I finally learned his name. He was 1st Lt. Brian Brennan from the storied 506th—the Band of Brothers Regiment—in the 101st Airborne Division.

Between the two wounded men, the entire blood supply of our small combat support hospital was gone within an hour. Resupply would not be possible until the weather cleared. Twice, the overhead "God Voice" sounded asking for blood donors and twice, hundreds of soldiers and civilians dropped everything and lined up to volunteer. Humanity at its finest, those volunteers were yet one more part of the enormous team that contributed to the outcome.

That night, Lieutenant Brennan was flown out to Bagram and then eventually to the United States. After he left, we were dejected and exhausted, knowing he had a very severe brain injury and had a high likelihood of suffering permanent damage, dying, or worse yet, being a vegetable for life. What did we save? Was it worth it? Would his family hate us? Would he?

We had followed all—okay, almost all—of the protocols. Every step along the way, we had done our very best, but what happens when you know in your heart of hearts that your best probably wasn't good enough?

For the next several weeks, we talked about the young lieutenant with his whole life ahead of him—or what was left of it—then he and his story were lost in the crush of patients and mass casualty events that followed and he became just one more face, one more sad story, in a busy deployment.

We found out later that Lieutenant Brennan had been in a coma at Walter Reed Hospital for several weeks, eyes open, but staring blankly, not recognizing even his own mother. He was in a near vegetative state, unresponsive to those around him, but then during this time, Gen. David Petraeus stopped by the hospital, making the rounds, talking with the wounded, consoling family members.

At Lieutenant Brennan's bedside, General Petraeus leaned in for a private pep talk with the unconscious lieutenant. Aware of the 506th's proud legacy, the general whispered the unit's motto: "Currahee." That simple word triggered a subtle movement from the comatose officer. In fact, General Petraeus and the family members weren't even sure they'd seen it. In a stronger voice, the general chanted, "One, two, three: CURRAHEE!" And immediately Lieutenant Brennan struggled to sit up, definitely responding to his unit's call to duty. Everyone who witnessed this improbable miracle cheered, some cried, and some prayed and gave thanks. No one would ever forget the miracle they witnessed that day.

From that day forward, his progress was simply astounding. Lieutenant Brennan remained in the Army, was promoted to captain, attended the Captain Career Course, got married, and became a company commander. Each step along the way has been a miracle, yet so magically normal.

Months passed and I was back in the United States. I first learned what had transpired almost exactly a year after the event when I was sent a link to a CBS *60 Minutes* report by David Martin. Watching the video, I was instantly transported back in time.

Army Lt. Brian Brennan. "I remembered Lieutenant Brennan so clearly: so helpless and so hurt, hanging in that shadowy place between life and death, with an entire medical team fighting for him who had no assurances there would be a good outcome. Seeing him alive was amazing." BRIAN BRENNAN PERSONAL PHOTO

I remembered Lieutenant Brennan so clearly: so helpless and so hurt, hanging in that shadowy place between life and death, with an entire medical team fighting for him who had no assurances there would be a good outcome. Seeing him alive was amazing.

I sat alone in my office and watched the CBS report once, twice, ten times with tears in my eyes, scarcely able to comprehend how far Brian had come. Walking and talking? And still serving in the Army? I couldn't wrap my brain around the magnitude of his improvement.

The team responsible for his outcome numbers in the hundreds and perhaps even over a thousand. It ranges from the soldiers and medics on the scene, the operations cells that gathered the information, the medevac and sister ship crews, the combat support hospitals at two locations, the Air Force air evac and critical care teams with their support and operations cells, Landstuhl and Walter Reed Hospitals, all of the therapists and volunteers, and so many more, including his family members who never gave up believing in miracles. And as for me, I learned never to count out a soldier with an indomitable spirit and an iron will to live.

—Lt. Col. Susan Fondy, MD

The night has a thousand eyes and often in a war zone there are evildoers out there, somewhere, lurking in the shadows, crouching in the underbrush, peeking over the ridgeline, waiting for an American patrol or a convoy to venture into the killing field.

Sometimes it's a sniper's bullet that does all the damage. It might be a trip wire that sets off a concealed mine. Or the simple ring of a cellphone that sparks an improvised explosive device. The weapons they use are often crude, but the result is the same . . . Last Rites, flag-draped coffins, and a funeral with full military honors. Some might say the less-fortunate are the ones who survive.

Marine in the Helmand

O ne of the Marines from the command post is beating the hell out of the trauma bell again, which is an oversized cut of rebar someone strung up just outside the tent at the back of our position—known as a forward resuscitative surgical team/shock trauma platoon—a few years ago. It's the one piece of our medical equipment that never fails. We all stumble grumpily and anxiously out of our tents into the afternoon glare of the Helmand Province in Afghanistan. I hear Sergeant G. two tents down, yelling, "Two Cat Alphas, ten mics out!"

In the front tent that serves as our emergency room, the teams are already in full motion, spiking IV bags and checking oxygen masks at the first two tables. No one is saying much. Everyone knows the drill.

I cut across to our operating tent. The corpsmen are moving fast. They have the instrument sets on the back table already open and the heater blasting. The trauma patients come in hypothermic, even though it is over 100 degrees outside. The air is close and tastes like a nosebleed. I am staring at the US flags each of us surgeons tied to the underside of the sagging ceiling over the OR table, when we took over from Alpha Surgical Team four months ago. I notice for the first time that the edge of my flag has bloodstains from our case last week, a failed attempt at a resuscitative thoracotomy.

That day, I had my hands around a young Marine's heart, doing cardiac compressions, while Hassan, our cardiothoracic surgeon, tried to repair the subclavian artery. We tried everything, but the damage around the great vessels was beyond repair and we never got a regular rhythm again. I called the time of death. While we were preparing the body for the honor flight down to Bastion, we rolled the patient and found a blood-streaked picture of him with his beautiful wife and children that

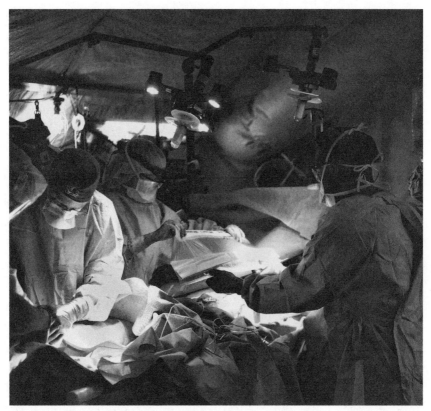

"In the front tent that serves as our emergency room, the teams are already in full motion, spiking IV bags and checking oxygen masks at the first two tables. No one is saying much. Everyone knows the drill." MARINE CORPS PHOTO

had fallen from his pocket. I refused to look at it, after two of my nurses left the tent in tears.

We draped the deceased in a new flag and waited for the attack squadron to position the Huey and the Cobra out in front. The whole FOB was there, lining the walk from the tent to the flight line. Until the birds spun up, it was nearly silent. We stood in two ranks facing each other and mourned the death of a Marine, a husband, a father. The sun sank lower toward the far range, the early foothills of the Hindu Kush. After the birds lifted away with our hero, we gathered the medical personnel for a debrief.

We had four more months to manage and the grief and anger were palpable. While I discussed and consoled, I suddenly felt the extent of my detachment and my fatigue. I needed to move on and get ready for the next trauma. And the cases kept coming.

"It's another double amp," Andy says walking into the OR, "just one, not two." He's my brother in here, my general surgeon co-operator. It's just the two of us this week and we're tired. "Marine, again," he says shaking his head and walking back out toward the flight line.

I cut back across to the communications tent to make sure the walking blood bank has been called. Chief beat me to it and there are already ten Marines sitting in the rec room watching a movie and rummaging through the community chow on the shelves. They are hoping to give some of their blood to one of their wounded brothers, hoping it won't ever be one of them who needs the same.

The docs in our lab tent have some blood product thawing. The dust-off medic called in the patient's blood type and our guys know what's going to save lives. I walk out front.

The litter teams are out, leaning against the earth and rock-filled fortifications that surround our medical complex, burning a few smokes before the chaos starts again. The corpsmen look like kids to me, scrawny and vulnerable under their boots, flak vests, and Kevlar. They are half my age. When I was twenty, I was pulling on oars on the Charles River, not pulling burned and bloodied men out of the back of a Black Hawk helicopter.

I watch them smoking and laughing and then I hear Sergeant G. yelling again, "Inbound, two mics." We can hear the two birds before we can see them, banking across the deep river wadi beyond the corner of our forward operating base. The Army dust-off crews fly missions together, and I will always revere the courage and the speed of their pilots and crews. "Line up!" somebody yells at the litter team, who are throwing on their goggles and Kevlar helmets.

Andy and I stand to the side with our backs to the protective barrier and watch the dust from the rotor wash blast through the opening as the Black Hawks touch down. The corpsmen are already running, crouched down under the blades. The medic comes across first and we lean in to hear him above the racket, ". . . foot patrol, IED blast, double amp, unstable, pulse 120s, still bleeding."

The team is back with the injured warrior, pale and dusty, eyes closed, grimacing, writhing, shards of femur and tibia scissoring on the gurney where his legs should be. I close my eyes, whisper a prayer, and follow him into the tent.

Life accelerates suddenly, my focus narrows. I am helping the corpsmen cut away what is left of our patient's cami uniforms and blast boxers. There are three tourniquets on each thigh and none of them are working on the right, where the blast has ruptured all the way up to the groin crease. I feel for the femoral pulse and jam my thumb down on it to stop the bleeding. There is a flurry of motion around me. I hear our patient grunt as a central line goes in and a second transfusion is started. "Talk to him, guys," I say to the nurse at the head of the bed. "Tell him he's going to be okay."

He was on a foot patrol, in Afghanistan's Helmand Province, when an IED nailed him. "Cat Alpha. Double amp . . ." was the radio transmission. By the time he was transported to the field hospital, the staff was ready for him.
MARINE CORPS PHOTO

His blood is warm across my thumb and I stare for a second at the tangle of muscle and bone distal to my hands and run the plan: ex-lap, iliac control, femoral artery ligation, above the knee amputation, through knee on the other side, package, call our medical upstream teams at Camp Bastion, ship him out. I lock eyes with Chief: "Start drawing from the walking blood bank, let's go to the OR."

Andy takes over for me so I can wash the blood off my arms, holding pressure on his groin as we walk him back to the OR tent. I notice our Marine's right ring finger and pinky are blown off and wrap his hand with Kerlex gauze. I switch back to the artery while Andy gets his gown and gloves on. The anesthesia team nails another rapid induction and intubation, while someone douses the abdomen with Betadine.

In my gown and gloves, under the two OR lights, I am sweating already. One of our corpsmen is jamming his thumb down on the femoral pulse, while we incise the abdomen. Andy has the belly open and I am holding intestines to the side while he exposes the iliac vessels. We pass the loops around the right, and then the left iliacs, and clamp them down. It's been about ten minutes since we got him in the tent. He's getting his twelfth unit of packed reds and his fourth fresh frozen plasma. We turn to his stumps. His base deficit is −27 and his pulse is in the 130s. Everyone takes a deep breath, but stays in motion.

The corpsmen help us scrub off the grime of dust and blood stuck to the stumps of his legs. The first few times we did this as a team, we were hesitant and slow, afraid that somehow our scrubbing would make worse the tangle of mud, tendon, and bone that was once a leg. Now, nonviable tissue is cut away decisively to prepare the stumps for the initial revision amputation and debridement. This is our fifteenth double amputation case. Tragically, we are now plenty experienced at this procedure.

While I work on the left limb and Andy works on the right, I am not thinking of our Marine's next five flights over the next week: first from our forward operating base to the big base at Camp Bastion thirty minutes south, to Bagram Air Base, then on to Landstuhl Army Hospital in Germany for a few days. Then a flying intensive care transport plane, stateside to Bethesda, then on to the Naval Medical Center in San Diego. I am not thinking of the next ten to fifteen painful surgeries he is bound

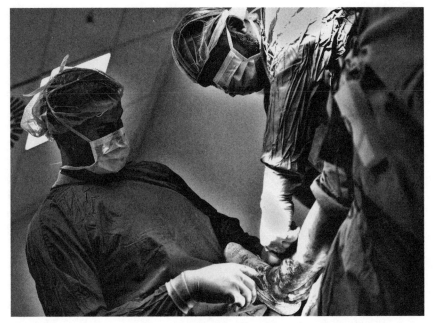

"I jam my thumb down on it to stop the bleeding. There is a flurry of motion around me. I hear our patient grunt as a central line goes in and a second trans-fusion is started. 'Talk to him, guys,' I say to the nurse at the head of the bed. 'Tell him he's going to be okay.'" AIR FORCE PHOTO

to have. I am not thinking of the first time he understands what he is missing or the first moment his wife and kids glimpse his limbs. I am not thinking of the painful hours and days and weeks he will spend standing and walking on his prosthetic legs. I am focused on finding the best tissue planes and saving the most length. I am intent on the femoral vessels as I dissect tissue around the posterior aspect of his knee. I am stick-tying the artery twice so it won't start bleeding again during his first flight to Bastion.

Blair and Spencer are transfusing the fourth unit of whole blood. Our Marine is rapidly improving. His pulse is steady in the 90s, and his base deficit is −6. Andy and I are done with his legs. Chief wraps a splint over the end of each stump, while I splint the Marine's hand and forearm. I rip off the blood-soaked gown and step into the relative cool air of the communications tent. Someone hands me an ice-cold Gatorade and I

As a C-130 medevac flight leaves the war zone, it deploys a spread of flares in case an insurgent gunner launches a heat-seeking missile at the defenseless transport. Its precious cargo is America's wounded warriors bound for Landstuhl Hospital in Germany, then on for further treatment stateside. AIR FORCE PHOTO

pound it down. Someone hands me a phone, and I tell the British trauma surgeon at Camp Bastion what to expect in thirty minutes. This is our formal hand-off. At Bastion, our Marine will get "proper" hospital care, CT scans, and wound vacuums for his stumps. Our work will be formally critiqued and improved upon, as it will be as he makes his way up the echelons of care.

Next week, we will huddle around the one landline in the tent and listen on speakerphone to the crackle and garble of the teleconference that connects us to each of the major points of care that our patients will travel through on their way home. We'll hear about the fractures that we missed and the evolving battle against infections and organ failure that takes hold of so many of our blast-injured patients.

If we're lucky, one of those many voices chronicling the medical evacuation process, maybe someone who has worked a small trauma tent like this one, will give us a small "Atta Boy!" for our first efforts in cheating death again.

Outside, on the flight line, it's dark as the litter team runs our Marine out to the Black Hawks. He is bundled carefully, and our flight nurse Jim knows his story by heart and is suited up and geared up for the ride. I slap him on the back, "Safe flight, Brother!" Andy and I watch them lift away and suddenly, the airfield is perfectly quiet, nothing but a dark expanse with a few small blue lights to mark the landing zones. "Cigar?" asks Andy. "Why not," I say. We head back to the tent to grab some folding chairs, jackets, and cigars. I almost feel relaxed . . . at least until the next time someone bangs on that trauma bell.

—Chris Dewing

America's war on terrorism, which has included combat in Iraq and Afghanistan, has led to numerous innovations in caring for our nation's wounded warriors. Moving field hospitals and aid stations closer to the front, often in the midst of the enemy, has improved survival rates. Dr. Yang Wang would lead a trauma team on the first airborne emergency room in Afghanistan, transporting critically wounded patients from remote forward operating bases to larger equipped and staffed military hospitals in country.

"Have You Ever Seen It This High?"

The first thing I noticed after arriving at Camp Bastion in Afghanistan was the dust. It was everywhere—creeping through every crevice into every tent, and caking our nostrils and tongues with each breath we took. While startlingly intrusive at first, over the next several months it slowly settled down and became just another part of the everyday minor aggravations. Just like the sweat that covered us day and night, except for the brief five minutes after a shower before the water evaporated; like the daily shaking booms from distant controlled-detonations of unexploded ordnances; or the too-often-a-day static blare of the overhead speakers announcing, in a hauntingly gentle female British voice, "Op-minimize, op-minimize, op-minimize," telling us of a brief shutdown of outside communications because another round of injured or dying soldiers had arrived from outside the wire by medevac. (All communications links—phone and internet—are cut until the next of kin of all casualties can be notified.)

This was my first deployment to Afghanistan, and I had been tasked as leader for the first tactical critical care evacuation team (TCCET) dedicated to fixed-wing air transport of combat casualties between the minimally staffed hospitals of forward operating bases and the three fully staffed advanced trauma hospitals at Bastion, Kandahar, and Bagram. The theory is that rather than spending excessive time and resources at the remote hospitals and aid stations providing definitive surgical care and post-surgical resuscitation before being transported to the larger hospitals, soldiers and Marines do better when they receive initial "damage control" procedures (amputations to control bleeding from limbs, tying off bleeding vessels, removing damaged bowel segments and spleens, packing bleeding livers to control bleeding from the torso, intubating the trachea to control airway and breathing, starting empiric medications to

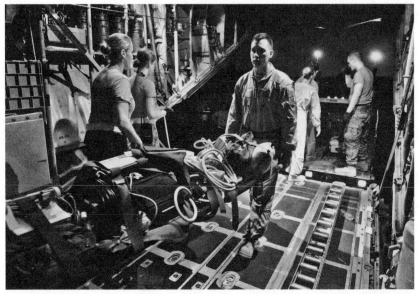

Loading equipment onto a C-130 transport plane to receive and evacuate wounded combatants from the war zones of Iraq and Afghanistan. The medevac flights carry the seriously wounded to Ramstein Air Base in Germany, then they are bused over to Landstuhl Hospital. AIR FORCE PHOTO

mitigate possible undiagnosed brain injuries where CAT scan machines are unavailable), and then are transported with ongoing resuscitation during their flights to larger trauma hospitals as quickly as possible. By decreasing time spent at the remote sites and getting the wounded to the more resource-rich medical centers earlier, morbidity and mortality rates have been dramatically cut.

So for five months in the blistering Afghan summer of 2012, we converted the dim blue-lit cargo hold of a C-130 transport plane into a mobile intensive care unit and flew back and forth across the entire country countless times providing resuscitative care to our nation's wounded warriors on their long journey back home.

One week into our arrival, we got our first mass-casualty call from a forward operating base (FOB)—seven patients needed to be transferred to Bagram. Five Marines and their Afghan interpreter had been injured by an improvised explosive device while they were on foot, and one soldier was injured in an unrelated helicopter crash. The injured included one Marine with 60 percent burns who was on a ventilator, two Marines with 20 percent burns also on ventilators, one Marine with a skull fracture and a collapsed lung on a ventilator, and one Marine with a penetrating neck injury on a ventilator, the Afghan interpreter with hip and lower back contusions and awake, and the soldier with a concussion and possible cervical spine injury who was also awake.

Our team consisted of two physicians—me and an internship-trained flight physician—two critical care nurses, one flight nurse, and two medical technicians.

In the air on our way to the remote FOB, we developed a game plan and prioritized the injured patients for order of transport. Given there were five ventilated patients, we would require two trips (we only had four portable ventilators available in the aircraft). We decided that on the first trip we would take the three burn patients and the one with the head and lung injuries. Then we would return for the remaining three. As the senior physician on the team, I assumed primary responsibility for what sounded like the most critical patient—the Marine with 60 percent burns.

After our plane touched down, we hopped in an ambulance, and headed for the hospital. We drove past tents and blast-walls with scattered American and Afghan soldiers watching us with cigarettes hanging out of their mouths and weapons slung across their shoulders, their outlines blurred by the haze of dust. The drive took a few minutes but it felt like an hour. My heart pounded with anticipation.

At the doorway into the hospital, we moved through a cluster of Marines in dirt-caked uniforms, and dust from their boots up to their teeth. They watched us take our equipment in without saying a word. I did not realize until later that those men watching us intently, silently, were all battle buddies of the casualties we were there to care for. Over the next five months, this same gathering at the entrance to other hospitals, with this same collection of somber faces, became all too familiar. But this being my first week into my first Afghanistan deployment and my first mission with multiple critically ill patients, I was too excited and too inexperienced to really see them for who they were or understand the reason they were gathered there.

Five Marines and their Afghan interpreter were severely injured when an IED detonated as they passed by. MARINE CORPS PHOTO

We split up to assess our patients, and when I walked up to my badly burned Marine, the surgeon came up to me and handed me a lab printout with a hemoglobin concentration of 26. "Have you ever seen it this high?" Normal hemoglobin ranges between 12 and 15. But when a burn victim no longer has enough skin to keep water from evaporating from the body, the hemoglobin concentration goes up.

Having gone through residency training at the northeastern Ohio regional burn center and Level I trauma center in Cleveland, I have seen burn patients before, and I have seen hemo-concentrations before. But here, at an FOB in the middle of Afghanistan, on my first real mission, printed on a piece of paper the size of a gas-station receipt, I find the worst hemoglobin concentration I have ever seen. The worst. Ever.

My patient was a Marine in his twenties, burned after the IED exploded next to him while he was on foot. All four of his limbs, his entire abdomen, and most of his face and head were wrapped in Kerlex bandages. An endotracheal tube protruded from his mouth squeezed tight by severely blue and swollen lips. Two catheters led into his groin—one placed into the femoral vein to pump in medications and fluids, and one placed into the femoral artery to continuously monitor his blood pressure. Three cardiac leads were attached to stickers stapled to his chest because the adhesive on the stickers had no dry skin to adhere to. A pulse-oximeter to measure blood-oxygen levels was clipped and taped to his tongue for lack of any other suitable site. I looked at his bedside, and the IV stand sagged under the weight of bags of intravenous crystalloid fluid, propofol, and fentanyl being infused to replace his fluid losses, for sedation, and for pain relief, respectively. He had been undergoing resuscitation for three hours by the time I arrived, and by that time his hemoglobin concentration had become an unfathomable 26.

I started to switch everything over to our portable equipment—cardiac monitor, ventilator, and fluid pump—and to calculate his hourly fluid requirement in accordance with our burn-management guidelines. It comes to about 2.5 liters per hour. I wonder if my pump can even be programmed for such a high rate. Twenty minutes after we arrived, one of my critical care nurses, Freddy, came over to report that his patient

It became a common scene outside aid stations and field hospitals in Afghanistan . . . battle buddies waiting for word that one of their own was okay. Sometimes the news was the worst. MARINE CORPS PHOTO

(intubated, with 20 percent burns) was stable, packaged, and ready to go. He saw me struggling to make sense of the tangled mass of tubing and wires going into my patient and asked if I wanted him to come back to help after he got his patient onto the aircraft. I gave him a very enthusiastic and grateful nod yes.

After another forty minutes, with Freddy's much needed help, my patient was packaged and ready to move. It took four medics, one on each handle of his litter, to keep him and all his attached equipment steady as we wheeled him to the ambulance, past that same silent group milling around the entrance. A total of six of us together lifted the three-hundred-plus pounds of patient and equipment into the ambulance. His platoon sergeant requested to come with us to the aircraft.

En route to the aircraft, things began to fall apart, one by one. First I lost his pulse-oximetry when the meter fell off his tongue and refused to reattach. Then the initially steady arterial blood pressure tracing

It took everyone to lift the patient and all the gear keeping him alive into the ambulance for transport from the aid station to the airfield. But even during the short ride, everything that could go wrong did, and he couldn't be loaded onto the evacuation flight until he was stabilized, which meant another trip back to the aid station. AIR FORCE PHOTO

degenerated into a flat line, and after trying to troubleshoot anything and everything we could think of, it never came back, leaving me guessing if the line failed or if the patient went pulseless. With his neck in a cervical collar and his arms and pelvis and legs all wrapped in bandages, I had no place to manually check a pulse. Finally, his expiratory carbon dioxide concentration tracing flattened and an equipment error message started to flash on the monitor screen.

By the time we arrived at the plane, the only data I still had to work with was a cardiac tracing because the stapled leads were still attached to his chest. I had no idea how he was oxygenating, what his blood pressure was (if he still had any), or if he was adequately ventilating (which was the job of the expiratory carbon dioxide monitor).

I was staring at a black box wrapped in layers of bandages with only a rise and fall of the chest to tell me that the ventilator was at least still delivering breaths into his lungs. Reluctantly I told Freddy this critically injured Marine could not get on a plane like that when I had no idea what was going on underneath his bandages. The ambulance dropped Freddy off to join the rest of the team and their three patients for the thirty-minute flight to Bagram.

I rode back to the field hospital with my patient and his platoon sergeant, who, throughout this whole trip to and from the aircraft, never took his eyes off his young Marine, and never spoke a word or asked a question. We arrived back to the hospital. Still not having said a single word, and with four medics on the ground supporting one end of the litter, the platoon sergeant carried the other end of the stretcher by himself back down off the ambulance. After the patient was safely unloaded, he walked back to rejoin his cluster of men who were still at the entrance, probably all wondering why their buddy came back when, more than any of the others, he needed to be on that plane.

Back inside the hospital, we disconnected everything from the patient, uncovered his groin and neck to check for a true pulse. I found one, although it was barely a thread. We gave him five pushes of adrenaline-like medications (phenylephrine and vasopressin) to augment his blood pressure while we replaced his arterial line, and we got back a reliable waveform and a good blood pressure. We started continuous infusions

Dr. Yang Wang (center) works with his team members on board a C-130 flying emergency room to stabilize a critically injured patient. The transport plane flew to remote air bases in Afghanistan, then flew the injured back to the larger field hospital at Bagram. AIR FORCE PHOTO

of the phenylephrine and vasopressin to ensure his blood pressure stayed up, adding two more infusion lines to the three that were already going into him. We replaced the defective CO2 detector with a new one and obtained a steady tracing. We exposed the tip of a burnt ear, attached a new pulse-oximeter, and got a reliable tracing. After an hour of work, he was finally stable again, and I spent another half-hour packaging him for transport, taking more care this time to ensure everything was secured, untangled, and functional.

When I finished, I stepped back and took in the view in front of me—a mass of five drips (propofol, fentanyl, phenylephrine, vasopressin, crystalloid fluid), three tubes (endotracheal tube, orogastric tube, urinary catheter), four lines (two peripheral intravenous catheters, one central venous catheter, one intra-arterial catheter), and Kerlex covering everything in between. The stretcher sagged under the weight of his body, a ventilator, a suction machine, two triple-channel fluid pumps, a cardiac monitor/defibrillator, and all the bags of medicines and fluids being infused.

Throughout the seven weeks of training leading up to this deployment, I had gradually become confident in my ability to easily handle anything that I was going to encounter. And after spending more than three hours trying to package up a single patient who kept threatening to die in front of me, I realized no amount of training could have prepared me for something like this.

On the flight line at Bastion Airfield in Afghanistan, Dr. Yang Wang and his medical team with their Alaska Air National Guard flight crew. In addition to treating American and Coalition troops, they also took care of Afghan soldiers and civilians. AIR FORCE PHOTO

The second transport to the aircraft went without incident, and the flight to Bagram was uneventful. We got him to Bagram warm, weaned off the phenylephrine, with stable vital signs, and making adequate amounts of urine (a sign of good end-organ perfusion). Still, he was far from out of danger, and despite our best efforts, I was not sure he would make it.

Two weeks later, during a teleconference, I heard he arrived at Landstuhl Regional Medical Center in Germany. Though he arrived there still intubated, he was displaying purposeful movements (a good sign of preserved brain function). He was still being prepared for his long flight to the burn center at Brooke Army Medical Center in San Antonio and the subsequent long road toward recovery and rehabilitation. I hoped he would see his family soon.

It has now been almost two years since I left Afghanistan. When I look back, I can still bring up vivid images of that critically burned Marine, as well as many of the other injured American, Coalition, and Afghan soldiers and civilians we treated. While I sometimes worry that I will not get a chance to write everything down before these memories fade, I am more convinced there is plenty of that Afghan dust still stuck on me that I may never be able to shake out.

—Dr. Yang Wang, ER Physician, Camp Bastion, Afghanistan

Military members often run into others they served with, trained with, and fought beside. These unexpected meetings occur almost every day, and every once in a while, something special happens.

For Army Col. Nick Cressy, his airport encounter with a wounded warrior he remembers from Afghanistan was bittersweet.

Reunion at the Airport

When I was with the 82nd Airborne Division from mid-2009 to 2010, I was involved with getting the right medical personnel, equipment, and assets in place to take care of our wounded warriors in Afghanistan. Those who couldn't be cared for in country were flown to Landstuhl Hospital in Germany. As such, every day our office, the Division Surgeon, checked the flight manifests of the medical evacuation flights from the previous day, and noted who was outbound.

Eighteen months later, I was stateside traveling in uniform and had a short layover in Dallas to catch another flight to San Antonio, home of Brooke Army Medical Center where many soldiers were rehabbing. While at the Dallas airport I noticed a young specialist approaching our gate. He had a very visible scar from the front to the back of his head. He came up to me and stood at attention until I said, "At ease trooper," then I asked him to sit down next to me. I asked if there was anything I could do for him and we chatted.

Eventually I asked when and where he was wounded and what happened. When he told me about his Alive Day—the day he should have died but didn't—I flashed back to a day in August 2009 when medevac helicopters picked up a critically wounded soldier shot in the head. I remember the soldier had been wounded while working in the operations center of his forward operating base when a bullet penetrated a wall of sandbags and nailed him. He wasn't wearing his Kevlar because the attack was in its early stages and he was in a secure bunker. It looked bad and our division surgeon didn't think he'd make it; he thought he might even die in transit, on the flight to Germany.

And now, sitting next to me at the Dallas airport is the guy we thought was not going to make it. He was walking with a slight shuffle,

"I noticed a young specialist approaching our gate. . . . He came up to me and stood at attention until I said, 'At ease trooper,' then I asked him to sit down next to me. . . . When he told me about his Alive Day—the day he should have died but didn't—I flashed back to a day in August 2009 when medevac helicopters picked up a critically wounded soldier shot in the head." MARINE CORPS PHOTO

a little slow putting his words together, but still walking around and returning from his trip to Disney World, all paid for by a wounded warrior group.

His mother was with him, and I could see that even though she was glad to have her soldier boy home and out of harm's way, she had a heavy heart, probably knowing what he would be facing for the rest of his life. I knew it too—he was one of the casualties of our war on terrorism—but I held off showing any emotion in front of him, waiting to break down until I got to my car at the airport parking lot.

—Army Col. Nick Cressy (Retired)

The mountains of Afghanistan disappear into the clouds, obscuring evil lurking in hidden caves, hunkered down behind rocks and trees, waiting for American foot patrols to wander into their killing field, for helicopters to fly within range of rocket-propelled grenades and shoulder-fired missiles.

Cliffhanger

Iwas a surgeon with a light infantry battalion of the 101st Airborne's 2nd Combat Team in the spring of 2011. We had been in Afghanistan since the previous summer. My physician assistant and I ran a ROLE I aid station, operating in the Kandahar Province in Afghanistan. I also went with the assault element on all the major missions. We had a cadre of combat medics in the aid station and in addition combat medics were assigned to each of the platoons.

Typically most doctors don't go out on patrols, but since I'm a prior infantry officer with Special Operations training and experience, I felt that I could contribute this way from the beginning of our series of missions. As it turned out, leadership at all levels liked to have me do this after I did it on our first mission. I had already done this during my five years in my previous Special Operations job. Combat medics do an extraordinary job, and I had already seen that with a critically injured patient, there were cases where it was very advantageous when I and several medics treated the worst casualties together. My experience was that the medics as well as the soldiers liked me to go out with them, certainly after the first time we had serious casualties, which occurred very soon after we started doing ground operations. I had one case where a medic seemed ambivalent about me being out there, but that particular mission ended up with a lot of casualties and he admitted immediately afterward how much he appreciated me being on the ground with him.

This was a three-day mission beginning with helicopter infiltration at around four o'clock that morning. As I remember there were two platoons, which were the main assault elements that would be clearing villages in this region of Kandahar Province. I was with one of the platoons. We arrived at the landing zone on schedule and moved out. By the time

Two platoons were dropped in to check local villages for insurgents and bomb-making materials. It was a three-day mission.
ARMY PHOTO

the sun was up on the first morning, the platoon I was with was making good progress clearing a village, interviewing village elders, and searching for evidence of weapons and supplies for producing improvised explosive devices.

At about 9:30 that morning, I was near the platoon leader's radio operator when he received a message about a traumatic amputation. Apparently the other assault platoon had a team up on a small mountaintop and one of those soldiers had sustained an IED blast and had his right leg blown off. Whoever was calling us requested I come to assist with the casualty.

The platoon leader sent one of his NCOs and a soldier to operate the Vallin (mine detector) with me and we set off at a run across uncleared fields toward the hilltop where the injured soldier was. Despite the danger of tripping a buried mine, we ran maybe five hundred meters, climbing over walls and cutting through compounds.

With all our gear on it seemed like we ran for an hour, but most likely it was around fifteen minutes. Since it was the beginning of the mission, we all were carrying a full load of water, food, ammunition, etc.—I also had my aid bag, my weapon, and seven liters of water—and it was difficult going as the temperature was getting up around 100 degrees already. I ran with the NCO and the mine-detector soldier for what seemed like forever. Finally we stopped where the other platoon was deployed. I looked around and shouted, "Where's the patient?"

"Up there," a soldier yelled, pointing straight up the rock, which was about three or four stories high. We all started clawing up the rock face. Unknown to us at the time, the platoon medic who had been with another squad at the time had just arrived at the base of the rock and started climbing up the other side. By the time we got to the top, with the weight of all the gear I was carrying and the heat, I was pretty spent. The platoon medic had arrived on top just a moment before I did.

One of our mortar men was laying almost at the apex of the mountaintop with his right leg amputated at mid-thigh. Not sure what type of munitions had exploded on top of that rock, but I doubt it was command detonated. Most likely it was a buried mine, with a pressure plate, or even something left over from previous conflicts.

It was a great vantage point for security and observation, so it's conceivable that an enemy would rig some kind of explosive up there to deny us the use of the location. I believe it exploded when the soldier stepped on it. One of his buddies had already put a tourniquet on the casualty's thigh, although he was still oozing blood.

"The platoon I was with was making good progress clearing a village . . . when we received a message . . . one of those soldiers had sustained an IED blast and had his right leg blown off." ARMY PHOTO

It was quite a climb, with full packs, just to get to the injured soldier on top of a ridgeline. Getting him down the sheer rock face was near impossible. ARMY PHOTO

The medic had just finished the IV and had the fluids running. I shouted to our injured soldier to wake up and felt his radial pulse which was weak and difficult to detect. I decided to start HEXTEND right away, at the same time. (HEXTEND is a colloid fluid, a complex carbohydrate solution that stays in the vasculature longer than isotonic fluids.)

I set up a FAST-1. (A FAST-1 is an intraosseous infusion device, which is for use in the sternum. It has a circle of needles and when pushed into the sternum, a center infusion needle fires from a spring into the bone.) This FAST-1 failed to fire, so I started a second IV and my medic and I ran two units of HEXTEND in almost together.

Our patient had improvement in his pulse and was more alert and in pain so we also pushed morphine, added combat gauze, more pressure on the dressings, and reinforced the tourniquet. Even simple procedures were difficult working on the apex of this dirty rock.

A radio operator was talking to a helicopter in the area, which was apparently getting low on fuel, and if we didn't get our wounded soldier to the bottom of the rock within five or ten minutes, the pilot was going to have to turn back to refuel and we would have to wait for another chopper. Our soldier couldn't wait that long. He needed to be on that bird immediately.

Everyone on top of the rock helped us put our soldier on a flexible litter, and we basically skidded him down the steep side of the mountain, with dust and clods of dirt flying everywhere, pummeling those on the ground below. I thought for sure we were going to miss our window to get him out, but we managed to get him down and on the helo before it had to leave the hasty landing zone at the bottom of the mountain.

He was flown out and we continued patrolling the area. Later that day we set up for the night in a strongpoint and heard over the net that during the night before, Osama Bin Laden had been killed on the raid in Pakistan. I was so excited about the turn of events, and once our perimeter was secure, I lay down and fell asleep within a minute or so of hearing the news! We also heard that our guy survived his critical injuries and was

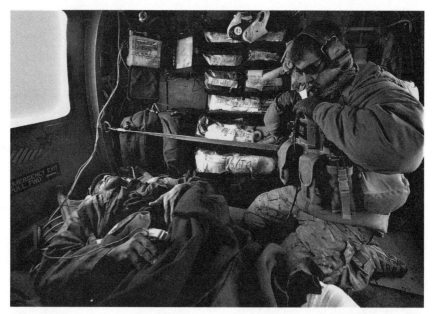

"We stabilized and evacuated well over a hundred trauma patients, and we packaged them so carefully to withstand the medevac flights that between our care and the terrific job all the flight medics did on board, I don't think we ever lost anyone in flight." AIR FORCE PHOTO

on his way to Landstuhl Hospital in Germany. In fact, throughout this tour we stabilized and evacuated well over a hundred trauma patients, and we packaged them so carefully to withstand the medevac flights that between our care and the terrific job all the flight medics did on board, I don't think we ever lost anyone in flight. On a personal note we had less than a month before we were due to fly home, and yet we were still at a horrendous up tempo!

I was pretty sure the reason why our battalion was continuing at this pace was because of our previous successes, resulting in our continuing to receive missions at this rate. Everyone was looking forward to the end of this year-long rotation, and I think the cumulative wear and fatigue was beginning to add up. However, I actually had mixed feelings about leaving in some ways. I wondered how other units would fare, especially as they went through the steep learning curve while getting proficient in this environment.

—Mack Easty

Everyone has a bad day at work, but with military doctors and nurses in a war zone, their "bad day" often ends with a flag-draped coffin loaded on an Air Force transport plane bound for the States.

Heartbreak in My "Dream" Job

For most of my thirty-year career we were not at war . . . things were quiet but we still prepared for eventual conflict. That day came when the New York Trade Center buildings came crashing down. I remember being on vacation in Garmish, Germany, with my family and while parked in a hardware store, a German man excitedly told us to turn on the radio, saying that the United States had been attacked. That was the most devastating day I can remember.

I was stationed in Aviano, Italy, at the time and I felt in my heart that being on vacation was the wrong thing to do, so we left for home immediately. The whole military community was stunned and scared. My units were imbedded in a small town called Sacile, geographically separated from the main base with a forty-minute response time for the Security Forces. Our units were locked down and from that day forward our guard was up every day.

Fast forward to 2006 when I reported to Ramstein Air Base in Germany for my "dream" job as the 86th Aeromedical Evacuation (AE) Squadron commander. We immediately increased our deployment opportunities and flew in and out of Iraq and Afghanistan on C-17 transports to pick up the injured. The design team for this aircraft had it right for AE . . . there was plenty of space, lighting, electrical capability, and oxygen for our patients. We would leave from Ramstein in the darkness with the back end of the aircraft filled with supplies, helicopter parts, MRAPS, and other supplies to keep the war machine running. Upon arrival at Balad Air Base in Iraq in the darkness, the loadmaster would quickly begin off-loading the equipment so we could rapidly reconfigure the aircraft into a flying hospital. On those missions we never knew the number or complexity of the patients we would fly.

Soon after arriving in country, the C-130 was off-loaded of supplies, munitions, and other necessities of war, then reconfigured for the influx of critically injured patients to be transported back to Ramstein Air Base in Germany, adjacent to Landstuhl Hospital. AIR FORCE PHOTO

The team was made up of three flight nurses and four enlisted flight techs (EMTs). We would also bring the critical care air transport teams, made up of one emergency trained physician, one ICU nurse, and one respiratory tech. As oxygen was being strung throughout the plane, the flight nurse was taking reports, gathering medications, and trying to make sense of this chaos.

There were times when operations were suspended as RPGs were incoming. We were sitting ducks on that plane, and all you could do was say a prayer that their trajectory was off and it would hit the dirt instead of your plane.

I remember one time when we flew in, it was hot and miserable. As the patients were being rapidly enplaned, one of the patients, a contractor, had been hit with an improvised explosive device (IED) and severely wounded. He was loaded onto the aircraft floor on an overweight litter due to his size and the fact that the litter stanchion was not stressed to hold his weight. My seat was right in front of him and the smell of his left leg stump was nauseating. It was made more aggravating when the flies started swarming. All I wanted to do was get airborne so we could cool off and recirculate the air.

On one mission, one of my patients was a young Army lieutenant who had just graduated from the US Military Academy and by all accounts was still recovering from his anesthesia. That is how fast they moved them out . . . the hospital wanted to always have the bed space in the event of a mass casualty. This young twenty-three-year-old had been on patrol with his unit and hit by an IED, losing his leg. There are so many like this young man that I saw on every AE mission I went on and it was heartbreaking. The statistics were the best of any war . . . 97 percent survival rate if they made it to a theater hospital. What we don't know is what the end result was. What kind of quality of life do these soldiers, airmen, and Marines have now?

During my deployment to Kandahar Province, Afghanistan, in 2012, I was the Aeromedical Evacuation Squadron commander and remember vividly that our days were never normal. The casualties came in every day without fail. As I watched them being hurriedly carried off the medevac helicopters to waiting ambulances, I knew only minutes earlier they had been in some sort of gun battle or were hit with an IED while on patrol. Watching from afar, it always saddened me to tears to think this patient was someone's son, husband, or father. Every day my medical flight teams of physicians, nurses, and technicians, along with critical care teams, set out to do what they do best . . . willingly putting themselves in harm's way in hostile territory to care for the injured.

One day in particular I assisted with the coordination of care at the Role 3 trauma hospital as the ICU team worked feverously on a young soldier who had been hit by an IED the day before. He sustained injuries in the blast that severely damaged his lungs, causing pulmonary hypertension that required maximum ventilator settings. His saturations were quickly dropping in spite of the high settings.

As I worked closely with the critical care team in the ICU, it was determined we needed additional expertise. The decision was made by the trauma surgeon to request "reachback" from the Department of Defense

"The casualties came in every day without fail. As I watched them being hurriedly carried off the medevac helicopters to waiting ambulances, I knew only minutes earlier they had been in some sort of gun battle or were hit with an IED while on patrol." AIR FORCE PHOTO

Lung Team at the Landstuhl Military Treatment Facility in Germany. We immediately classified this movement as an "urgent" and set about requesting the team of eight specialists to stop their clinical duties and prepare for the eight-hour flight to Afghanistan in order to save the life of this young man.

I believe, even to this day, the American public will never know and understand all the stops that were pulled out on a daily basis to save the lives of our soldiers, airmen, and Marines, no matter the cost. You just can't put a price on saving someone's life. The survival statistics of Kandahar's Role 3 Hospital (NATO's term for a trauma center) were unheard of in previous wars. If an injured soldier made it to their hospital, they had a 99 percent chance of survival; many lived but so many died.

While waiting for the Lung Team to arrive, the ICU nurse called for help. This was a brave twenty-year-old Army man who was fighting the Taliban in a country struggling for survival, and right now as his heart stopped, he was struggling and fighting for his own life. After quick administration of epinephrine, bagging, and chest compressions, his heart was restarted. It was our job to keep him alive long enough for the Lung Team to arrive so they could provide the specialized care he desperately needed.

When the message came in that the Lung Team had arrived from Germany, I rushed to the flight line to greet them and urgently relay the patient's grave status. With the Lung Team at his bedside, the patient's heart stopped for the second time in forty-five minutes. Prompt chest compressions and several doses of epinephrine restarted his heart. Sadly, as the Lung Team prepared the setup for the Novalung equipment, his heart stopped for the third time. (Note: The Novalung was developed by German medical cardiac/lung specialists. This device was a pumpless lung assist device used by the Department of Defense Landstuhl Lung Team with a high success rate for recovery.)

This time chest compressions and epinephrine were not enough and the patient's fight to live was lost. His death was called at 0932. Everyone stopped in their tracks and the room went eerily quiet as eyes swelled up with tears. The Novalung was our only hope. Our soldier was dead and all of our advanced medical care could not bring him back. There was not a dry eye in the room. We felt defeated, helpless, and exhausted by all of the death, dying, and maiming this war had caused.

The following day, as I entered the hospital compound, the flag-draped coffin was being honored during the move from the morgue to the transport vehicle. Our patient was a Military Police K-9 handler, with a specialty in explosives. His working dog, a German shepherd, stood obediently beside another handler. The coffin moved by a group of hospital staff lined up in formation, standing at attention to pay their last respects and honor this brave man. It was hard to imagine what this dog was thinking. His companion was gone and would never come back.

It's been almost three years since I left Afghanistan. I didn't have to go because I was back at the clinic as a chief nurse, but I felt like I wasn't finished and had so much experience to share. I had seen a lot of death

" . . . as I entered the hospital compound, the flag-draped coffin was being honored during the move from the morgue to the transport vehicle. Our patient was a Military Police K-9 handler, with a specialty in explosives. His working dog, a German shepherd, stood obediently beside another handler. The coffin moved by a group of hospital staff lined up in formation, standing at attention to pay their last respects and honor this brave man. It was hard to imagine what this dog was thinking. His companion was gone and would never come back." AIR FORCE PHOTO

and dying in my three years as the 86th AES commander and again two years later. I think that was why I may have fallen into a depressive state a year later, and I still wonder if I have posttraumatic stress disorder. That is something I will eventually sort out, but in the meantime, my heart is saddened by the men and women we have lost since 9/11, and I hope and pray the ones who were injured have recovered and know that they have served their country well.

On a side note, I just took a Red Cross CPR Instructor class and one of the other students was an Iraq Army veteran who was in a wheelchair and paralyzed from the waist down. We talked a lot about the war, and we both were comforted with the similarities of the jobs we did while supporting OEF/OIF. He is now a CPR instructor, teaching at local firehouses and the EMT program at a local community college.

—Col. Elizabeth Cowles Harrell (Retired)

When severely wounded patients are airlifted out of the war zone and on to Landstuhl Regional Medical Center in Germany, critical care nurses such as Michelle Imlay endure the emotional toll of changing the bandages of burn victims, consoling amputees, and bridging the communication gap with Coalition troops from other NATO forces.

War Bonds!

During the summer of 2010, I had the incredible honor to care for the wounded and sick while stationed in Germany at Landstuhl, the premier trauma hospital that received the wounded and sick from Iraq, Afghanistan, and other parts of the Middle East, Africa, and Europe. A service member could be wounded on the battlefield and be in Germany in six to seven hours. This trauma system spanned three continents: Asia, Europe, and North America.

The fighting season was in full rhythm the summer of 2010 with flights to and from all three continents, which created surges in the numbers of wounded that impacted the medical wards. It was like a bus stopping outside of an emergency room with all critically ill patients and your wait-time for your run-of-the-mill closed small bone fracture had ballooned from four hours to twenty-four hours before the nurse could ask you why you were at the ER.

Almost all battlefield casualties are injured more than the usual "critical" patient in your average United States emergency department. Not to say there is not pain and suffering in stateside hospitals. It is just different. I have worked emergency rooms, in a step-down cardiac unit, ICU (neurological, medical, and trauma) and by comparison the war hospital surges were very different from anything I had ever experienced. An "easy" patient would have only one limb missing or not working due to injury, and a "hard" patient might have two or three limbs not working or missing, as well as complicated wounds or chest tubes.

Please do not misunderstand my intention with the use of such terms as easy or hard. In a nurse's mind these terms are equated with the amount of time needed to care for the patient. As an example, an "easy" patient could care for himself or herself, and only need some assistance such as help to get out of bed, or bathing and dressing with a wound that needed bandage changes, and a "hard" patient needs help with almost everything.

In the nurse's mind, "hard" equals a large amount of time, man-power to make sure all wounds, tubes, medications, bathing, eating, and charting are completed within the time allotted. A typical assignment for your twelve-hour shift would be two "easy" and three "hard" or four "hard" and one "easy" patient. And time sometimes had to be allotted for unseen events such as the wheelchair race between two Marines with pain medication on board that ended up in a crash with tubes, dressings, and IV lines all tangled in a large mess, or when one of your patients needs to return to the operating room for complications and will need closer observation when returned back to the hospital ward.

The number of patients assigned per shift would vary related to "easy" and "hard," but on many occasions we would help each other throughout the long days or nights. Often our NATO patients would stay longer for many reasons depending on the country of origin, type of wounds, and complications, and many times you would care for the same ones for continuity of care.

It was the "fighting season" and everyone knew there would be an increase in firefights . . . and with it, casualties. ARMY PHOTO

One room we called little NATO, because all the soldiers in the room were from the same NATO country with only one able to speak English and their native language. Many times things would take some time to translate from nurse to patient and then from the patient who spoke English to the other patients who only spoke their native language.

On one day while caring for the patients in little NATO, I was working with an Air Force nurse and I was asked by the patient why we were wearing different uniforms. We explained the difference between the Army and the Air Force, rank insignia on the uniforms, training, and all. As the patient translated to his colleagues, there would be periods of conversations between the patients while we worked. We talked about places we grew up, parts of the United States of America, and that I had been to their country while in college hiking in Europe and rock climbing in the mountains.

Then the patient asked the Air Force nurse if she had been to their country. "No," she replied, but "My grandfather had been a pilot during World War II and had been to their country and parts of Europe after bombing the hell out of Germany!"

We all started laughing and then when the translation made it all around the room, we were all laughing loudly and for quite some time. Others on the ward wanted to know what was so funny, stopped what they were doing, and looked in the room, trying to see something funny on such a long busy day. Well for me, the Air Force nurse had always been very proper, and that was the first time I heard her use any such language, even in the heat of some difficult situations. And for the soldiers, the story helped to relieve tension through laughter, and knowing Americans could laugh with them created a bond between warrior and nurse.

One patient whom I cared for many days during the very busy summer was in bad shape. He was also from a NATO country. When people are injured by IEDs, many variables are involved in how they sustain the injuries and the severity of the injuries, which include: how close to the blast they were; what kind of clothing they were wearing; if they were inside or outside of a building; and what type of "stuff" was in the bomb.

This soldier's injuries came from an IED, and with the help of one or two other medics or nurses, it would take about two hours to change the dressings on his legs: hip to ankles, all around the entire circumference of his limbs. His dressings would have to be changed twice a day, and the projectile injuries that can best be described as index finger–size indentation wounds one to two inches deep would need to be packed with dressings to help kill the bacteria that could cause him to lose his legs if not controlled.

His skin had been torn off by the sheer force of the blast so his legs looked like raw meat, and in places more like hamburger. The dressing changes involved a very slow process of unwrapping, unpacking, repacking, and then rewrapping his legs with several layers of bandages to help protect the fragile tissue.

Now this sounds very simple; however, it is not like changing a Band-Aid on your arm or leg or other superficial wounds.

Imagine a severe sunburn to both of your legs front and back with a severe "road-rash" with your skin peeled off and pocked every four to five inches, with penetrating wounds that go deep into your muscles, with oozing blood and serum saturating your gauze as you try to slowly remove it, bit by bit. Moment by moment, gauze piece by gauze piece, minute by minute that turns into hours that seems like days not only for the patient but also for the caregivers.

There's the smell, not only from the bacteria that is dead from the antibiotics given intravenously, but also from blood, muscle, pus, fear, sweat, and burn tissue all filling your olfactory senses without a saturation or numbing point. The pain for the soldier was matched only by my emotional pain of hours of feeling like this mad torturer who was inflicting pain by slowly removing strand after strand of gauze soaked with serum, blood, dead tissue, dried blood, and dead bacteria.

The smell of fear, morphine, blood, and sweat from the patient and the smell of my own fear and sweat filling my nostrils all carried an emotional traumatic force equal to the initial blast, burning a traumatic memory into my brain. Pain. Even after giving the maximum amount of pain medication via all the routes possible (IV and oral), calculating the time of maximum benefit of the onset of analgesia, begging the surgeon for some magical pill or procedure to prevent the pain-inducing process of dressing changes, reading as much as I could about ways to prevent pain, infection, and tissue healing to no avail, there was no answer other than "this is the process."

As one of the more senior nurses, some of the "hard" patients would fall under my care during my duty shift. Due to the physical pain for him and the emotional pain for me, we formed a painful bond. This bond was also filled with dread not only for him but for myself as the time for dressing change would approach; not only would his blood pressure elevate as the hour approached, I could feel my blood pressure elevate and the feeling of inflicting pain upon him was weighted with emotions, the sights and sounds of a busy fighting season, of eighteen-hour days with few reasons to celebrate on off days.

The seemingly endless days of war trauma wounds, of young faces

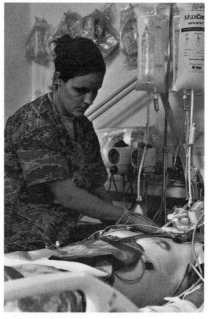

"His dressings would have to be changed twice a day and the projectile injuries . . . would need to be packed with dressings to help kill the bacteria that could cause him to lose his legs if not controlled." AIR FORCE PHOTO

bloodstained, mixed with months of Afghani dirt that smells very different from Iraqi dirt on the bodies of our wounded (I was able to tell which front they were from—Iraq or Afghanistan—just by the smell of the soil on the service member's body or uniform), for many of them would not have the opportunity to bathe for months on end while in the thick of the fighting. Given this fact, the dirt rich with bacteria and then a wound that would be speckled by all kinds of bacteria, we all feared infections that would "take" the badly injured arm or leg after days of attempting to kill this relentless enemy living in the battle wound with a "super-soup" of antibiotics. The fear of this enemy not visible by the human eye created medical tension to keep the wounds as clean as possible even during these long dressing changes, such that the changing of gloves would occur often, creating a pause in the dressing changes and a brief respite from the smells of war.

Then back to the task at hand. Conversations during dressing changes were usually absent due to my emotional pain and his physical pain; statements of "you need to keep breathing, do not hold your breath, breathe with me as I count 1, 2, 3" were a reminder to focus on something other than the pain. Many women know this from childbirth, athletes know this from training to "run" through the pain, pushing their brains to focus on everything else but pain, and warriors know this, but even the best of us are sometimes flooded with such overwhelming pain of the heart or body that we need someone to help us through our pain. That is why suffering is worse than pain. It is relentless emotional pain that is all consuming. The sharing of pain reduces our suffering and allows others to help with our burden. The mere memory of severe emotional pain can kill over time. It causes a burden on the body and it is more than the body can take. All kinds of chemical reactions deep within our tissue due to chronic emotional stress cause unseen physical stress that can result in heart attacks.

The sharing of emotional pain helps the healing process and can boost your immune system in the long run; however in the acute situation, our shared pain only created moments of sheer emotional panic, distracted by fierce duty to help win the war against the microscopic enemy in the soldiers' wounds. The flooding of all my senses, heightened by sleeplessness, long work hours, and the smell of foreign soil, blood, pus, urine, fear, antibiotics, body sweat, male soaps, and shaving cream, all seemed to peak with this soldier and his arduous dressing changes.

Maybe it was because he was my patient for many days while he was at the hospital, or because he was in a room by himself without the humorous-loving distractions of other warriors. Warriors provide this distracting-loving-care for each other during times of need that is unparalleled to anything I have ever seen or witnessed in civilian nursing. The comfort of a helping hand, a pat on the back, a muscled arm to help lift another warrior out of the bed to then place in a wheelchair, all the while balancing on one leg or using their half arm to steady one without legs, the humorous-loving-care grappling of chest tubes when someone is falling or helping to shave another who lost his hands—warriors provide comfort and care with no words, and the true understanding of each other's burdens.

The brotherhood warriors give to each other is more amazing than words can describe. The feeling of taking care of such amazing warriors was such a humbling gift. I would never replace the best and hardest year of my life, and I would never rob myself of the memory of taking care of "The One."

—Michelle Imlay

Air Force Critical Care team members realize there are no "typical" patients, especially for the most seriously wounded. And sometimes, no matter how much trouble-shooting they do, the Peter Principle—"if something can go wrong, it will go wrong"—throws roadblocks in their way, when precious minutes are wasted trying to transport that patient to the next care facility.

"Cat Alpha—GSW to the Head"

By July, we were two months into our deployment as an Air Force tactical critical care evacuation team, flying out of Camp Bastion to any forward operating base (FOB) with a landing strip long enough for a C-130 to land, getting critically injured patients from minimally staffed field hospitals to one of the three tertiary medical treatment facilities (MTFs) clustered in south/southeastern Afghanistan. We had flown enough penetrating head injuries that we were pretty well versed in the routine. These patients are almost always on a ventilator. While none of the FOBs have a CT scanner, so we never have any idea of the extent of intracranial injuries, common themes have emerged in our approach to these patients.

Information to get from the sending team: What was the GCS at presentation? Any paralytics given? Are T and L spine cleared so we can elevate the head of the bed (HOB)? Vent settings? Last arterial blood gas (ABG) values? Endotracheal tube position and size? Orogastric tube placed?

Things to get set up before we land: detachable back-rest that fits onto the transport stretchers to elevate the head to 30 degrees; 3 percent saline bolus and drip preprogrammed into the IV pump; phenylephrine, propofol, and fentanyl drawn up into syringes for push-doses as needed.

Things to get from the FOB before takeoff: "ketofol" mixed up and started (100 mg of ketamine injected into the 100mL bottle of 10mg/mL propofol) to maintain sedation; functioning arterial line to know when to push phenylephrine; a free-flowing IV line for boluses of as needed meds separate from IVs that are already infusing maintenance medications.

And then there are things that we'll make up as we go along.

Every flight required a different checklist of things to load, depending on the injuries of each patient they would be transporting. AIR FORCE PHOTO

So we hop into our aircraft, and thirty minutes later we've landed. We expected an ambulance to meet us and instead we find a couple of jeeps. It's me, my two critical care nurses, a distinguished visitor (DV)— the Army in-theater en route care director (one of the many amazing colleagues I met in the sandbox). We split ourselves and our litter full of patient movement items (PMI)—a SMEED, a vent, a triple-channel IV pump, a Zoll cardiac monitor/defibrillator—between the two vehicles and make our way to the medical tent. On the way, I look back at the amount of space behind our seats and wonder how we're supposed to fit a supine full-size patient into one of these vehicles. As if reading my mind, my driver tells me that their two ambulances are down and they have an MRAP (Mine Resistant Ambush Protected) vehicle waiting at the tent ready to move the patient.

We arrive at the tent and walk past the familiar collection of soldiers that have greeted us at other tents at other FOBs, dusty, bearded, with flat affects and staring eyes. There were more people inside. Ours is the only patient in the whole place. We meet the "ER" physician—he's a cardio-thoracic surgeon by training—and he tells me for the months he's been here, he has yet to do any thoracic cases.

The patient is an American soldier, Special Operations. Single gunshot wound into the forehead and out of the back, where the exit wound has been packed heavily with rolls of Kerlex to stop the bleeding. He is intubated and sedated. Apparently on arrival he was given a GCS of 6 because he did withdrawal to pain. He is on a propofol drip. His heart rate and blood pressure are normal—not too low, not too high.

We put an arterial line in, and we start hypertonic saline. We do not undo the dressings to his head, and I wonder if there's any point in the hypertonic saline when he already has a traumatic craniotomy. We prop him up to 30 degrees with our backrest to decrease intracranial pressure. We keep the C-collar on to keep his head midline to avoid any inadvertent internal jugular vein compression. We titrate down his fraction of inhaled oxygen to conserve our oxygen supply. We change his tidal volume and respiratory rate around to keep his peak pressure below 30 and his end-tidal CO_2 below 40. His base deficit is high, and his hemoglobin is low, so we start red blood cells and fresh frozen plasma. The whole process takes about thirty minutes and our distinguished visitor is more than happy to help with the packaging.

While we work, an Army medic makes his way to the bedside and starts asking questions. Eventually we find out he's the one that provided care on the ground at the time of injury, and he's the one that called dustoff (Army medical evacuation helicopter). He's caked in dust up to his teeth, and a large bloodstain covers the lower part of his top and the upper part of his pants. There is dried blood on his hands and under his fingernails. He has an expressionless face, and he keeps his eyes on the patient when he asks questions and answers ours. He makes a few trips between us and the group gathered on the other side of the tent watching us, and I am glad he's doing the talking for us while we work.

We are ready to go, and we get a call from our aircraft—one of the engines is down, and we are grounded. Unsure if it can be repaired. Great.

Unhook our oxygen tank, put the patient back onto the aid station's IV pump, ventilator, and monitor to conserve our batteries, and let's see what happens.

During the whole wait, our patient's condition stays rock stable. We find out a little more about the situation. The patient's group was caught

"The patient is an American soldier, Special Operations. Single gunshot wound into the forehead and out of the back, where the exit wound has been packed heavily with rolls of Kerlex to stop the bleeding. He is intubated and sedated. . . . He is on a propofol drip. His heart rate and blood pressure are normal—not too low, not too high. We put an arterial line in, and we start hypertonic saline. . . . We prop him up to 30 degrees with our backrest to decrease intracranial pressure." AIR FORCE PHOTO

in a firefight. He got shot with the medic right next to him. The patient was unresponsive, and the medic had nothing to offer except pressure to the back of the head to prevent further bleeding. The medic called for dust-off almost immediately. Dust-off arrived within minutes, but circled for another forty-five to sixty minutes because the landing zone was still hot with active shooting. During that hour of watching dust-off circling over his head, the medic made repeated calls for a landing, including one along the lines of threatening to shoot the helicopter down if it still wouldn't land. This comment apparently did not go over well with the dust-off colonel on the ground listening to the chatter.

We spend about an hour and a half trying to figure out how to get our patient to Kandahar. Option one—send the second HC-130 transport plane (we have two) with a maintenance crew, drop them off to work on the first one, and pick us up and take us the rest of the way. Option two— use dust-off for the rest of the trip, which means pickup, then a tail-to-tail with a second helicopter (due to distance), and then dropoff at Kandahar. Option three—see what the flight engineer can do to patch up the engine and make the aircraft fly. Option three finally comes through for us, and we are ready to take our patient to our aircraft.

So we wheel the patient with all the equipment attached out to the front door, and I see the MRAP that's waiting. Instead of an ambulance where the back door is about two-and-a-half feet from ground level and three-people wide, this back door is over four feet off the ground, and one-person wide. Awesome. We scramble him inside with a lot of grunting, straining, and hoping we would never have to do this again.

The Army medic comes with us for the transport. He hasn't said a word since we finished packaging the patient. One of our medics gives him some water and a Clif bar for nourishment. He drinks the water, and takes a bite from the bar. Our medic tries to start some conversation.

Once stabilized at the aid stations, patients are loaded, then stacked and racked for the flight downrange. AIR FORCE PHOTO

I can't hear anything over the humming of the plane, but it looks like a one-sided conversation. His eyes are fixed on a spot on the floor and he manages a nod once in a while.

We land and get the patient into the ER, and the medic is escorted away with an Army officer. I think it has something to do with what he yelled to dust-off when he was on the ground being shot at while holding a broken and bleeding head in his lap.

The ER doc who received the patient gives me a very skeptical look when I tell him about the patient's GCS—withdrawing to pain—and proceeds with the typical assessment, which is to strip him of all his drips and start from scratch. No need for input from the transport team. No ketofol, no 3 percent saline. Sure enough, his left leg starts to move again. The ER doc throws a look in my direction and lets out a "GCS 6" between his teeth. Yup, I'm watching, and yup, I heard you. We finish cleaning our equipment, and I see them taking him to CT.

We don't have another mission waiting for us, so we all go back to CT to see what actually happened inside his head. We stand behind the neurosurgeon and the radiologist and watch as the images come onto the screen in real time, and it looks like fireworks. Between the scatter of bullet fragments, there are intraparenchymal and intraventricular bright whites, and there are every shade of subdural and subarachnoid grays. As the images come through, the neurosurgeon starts to swear under his breath and before the scan is done, he gets up to get the OR ready and we go back to our plane.

Our engine still needed repair, so we spend another four hours that night on the flight line. We watch the flight line lights flicker in the distance, the C-17s and C-130s landing quietly, and the bombers launching with a roar. We eat deli meat and bread and cookies from take-out boxes from the dining facility. We drink Rip-Its. We fly back to Bastion. We keep working. A week later, during a teleconference, I learn he got started on the T3 protocol and got flown to Germany, and his family will be waiting for him there one last time.

I remember the patient, but I remember this mission more for the medic: the look of him, covered in dust, lips cracked, teeth yellowed, and beard caked in mud and dirt, sitting in the back of our C-130, looking at his patient, intubated, sedated, with an enormous amount of Kerlex wrapped around his head, and having to remember earlier sitting with him in his lap for a full hour after the initial injury, watching dust-off circling overhead and powerless to do anything to help the guy. I don't know what happened to him after he got to the field hospital.

The more of these things I write, the longer they become, and it seems like the more "nonmedical" details I want to write down. When I started work at a community hospital here in the Bay Area this summer, one of the first patients I treated was a thirty-something Hispanic man who came looking for help for anxiety. He told me he was an Army Airborne combat medic in Iraq.

He separated three years ago, got a job in an ER, and couldn't work after a few weeks because he couldn't cope with what he was seeing on a daily basis. He divorced. He had nightmares regularly, and woke most nights drenched in sweat. He was admitted to the county psychiatric ward last year because his family found him drunk, in his backyard, dressed in full combat armor, yelling at the sky about casualties that needed to be moved. His eight-year-old son woke him up one night because he was yelling and kicking in his sleep while they were sharing a bed. He had no idea what was wrong with him, but he said he came for help because he still doesn't have a job, and he doesn't want his son to think he's a "nut." I almost cried.

—Dr. Yang Wang

CONCURRENT
MISSIONS

When conflicts flare in distant parts of the world, Americans answer the call for help, whether it's dispatching combat units to restore order, or requesting medical personnel for humanitarian assistance.

The following few stories shine a spotlight on our military medical personnel in very difficult situations—from prepping an American soldier's body for burial after he was killed in a terrorist bombing in Berlin, to treating naval personnel after both undersea and aerial mishaps, to humanitarian missions to Liberia, Kosovo, and Somalia. These unexpected calls for help often occur concurrently with the continuing war on terrorism, as American combat units are deployed downrange, in Iraq and Afghanistan, and stationed in Korea—which is always a potential flashpoint.

~~

Pulling an all-nighter as duty officer is typically boring as hell, checking the hallways and the grounds outside every hour more to stretch the legs and get some fresh air than to look for intruders. But for Deb Berthold, what happened more than twenty-five years ago is a night she can never forget, still as vivid to her as if it unfolded just yesterday.

A Quiet Conversation

For every service member—enlisted, NCO, or officer—there are some drudgeries of military life that cannot be avoided. In basic training it's KP, or kitchen police, and fire watch, fighting to stay up at night while everyone else is snoozing. For me it was my turn as administrative officer of the day at the Army hospital in Frankfurt, Germany, one night in 1986. On any normal night, it would require walking the grounds and the hallways with a sergeant, ensuring doors that should be locked are locked, escorting meandering patients back to their rooms, making mundane notations on the duty log. Nothing exciting.

As the hospital dietitian I wasn't exactly an imposing deterrent to anyone who might wish to storm the compound. I only hoped the young sergeant pulling watch with me that night was trained in hand to hand if it was required. Neither one of us though was trained to deal with what would unfold later that night.

There was a news bulletin that said the La Belle discotheque in Berlin had been bombed. It was a popular hotspot for off-duty service members, which is why it was targeted. Initial reports said that hundreds were wounded, but then we learned that two had been killed instantly—a twenty-one-year-old Army sergeant and a young Turkish woman. (A few months later another soldier died of his injuries.) Anytime one of our own is wounded or killed anywhere, it hurts, but for me, I was pregnant and I immediately thought of that young soldier's mom.

Little did I know at the time, but part of our duties that night was to receive the deceased soldier from Berlin and ensure he was "prepared" to be sent back to the States for burial. The body was flown from Berlin's Templehof Airport to Rhein Main in Frankfurt, then brought to us via military ambulance. As we stood there at the receiving dock, my sergeant and I had no idea what to expect. We knew one of our own was coming in, but I guess I never realized the damage a point-blank bomb blast can do to a human body.

The ambulance pulled up and my first shock was seeing the sealed body bag. Minutes later, as we unzipped it, the smell of burnt flesh was overpowering. His head was wrapped in a plastic bag and his gold necklaces were embedded in the charred skin. His body was not intact, and we had to make a notation, including a list of all his personal effects.

I maintained my professionalism, but kept constantly thinking of this young soldier's mom, who would never again hug her baby. I carefully removed the bag from his face, and with respect and reverence, I cleaned him as gently as I could. It took me hours, and I asked him where was he from? And did he have any brothers and sisters? He was only a few years removed from high school, so I asked if he'd played sports. He looked so young, certainly too young to die. And was there anyone special in his

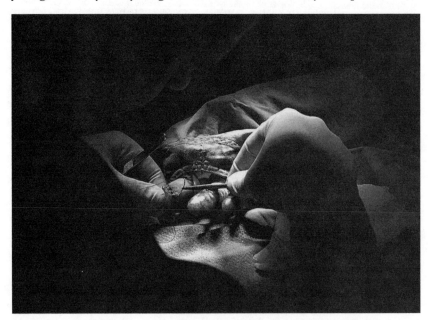

A terrorist bombing took his life. She had the difficult task of prepping his body for the trip home. ". . . constantly thinking of this young soldier's mom, who would never again hug her baby . . . I tried to make him as presentable as possible. . . ." NAVY PHOTO

life? (I hoped there wasn't, because I feared she would not be able to handle the loss.)

We spent hours together that night, and even though I knew he couldn't say anything, I asked what his favorite sports teams were. And why did he join the Army? Of course I made up his responses, as if we were having a quiet conversation.

I carefully dug out those gold chains from his neck and chest, not wishing to cause him any more

It took nearly all night as she carried on a conversation with the young soldier, fighting back tears, knowing his mom would never get to hold her baby again." She placed all of his personal effects in a plastic bag to accompany the body home. ARMY PHOTO

pain, and I tried to make him as presentable as possible. My battle buddy that night contacted the soldier's first sergeant in Berlin so we could get all of his ribbons and awards on his uniform, which accompanied him to the funeral home stateside.

I did not understand the process at the time, so I wasn't sure when this fallen warrior's family would actually "see" him, but I tried to make him look as peaceful and cared for as I could, in the event they were there when he arrived the next day. It took practically all night, and I was exhausted by the time I said goodbye to him, not really knowing who he was, but I knew I would never forget him. In the days after the bombing, Libyan terrorists took responsibility.

This young sergeant did not fall on a battlefield, but he died for the same reason our warriors are on distant battlefields today, the same reason our citizens are dying on our own streets, and the same reason there is a memorial where the Twin Towers once stood. That reason is known simply as terrorism.

Several days after the bombing, Armed Forces Network in Germany broadcasted a basic training graduation photo of my sergeant. And finally, that is when I cried. The handsome face on the screen looked nothing like the young man I spent hours with in the depths of Frankfurt hospital. Soon after, *People* magazine featured him and quoted his mom, who said the mortician needed a lot of wax and makeup to reconstruct his hand-some face, which had been badly burned in the bombing. Though it's been more than thirty years since that night, there is barely a day that goes by when I don't look at my own handsome son, feel blessed to have him and hug him whenever I want, and then I remember "my sergeant." And I wonder if his mom thinks of him as often as I do. But of course she does.

—Army Col. Debra D. Berthold (Retired)

Submarines are intended to glide through the oceans, silently, undetected, like a teardrop in a rainstorm. They can lurk offshore in enemy waters and no one even knows they're out there, then vanish without a trace, pop up half a world away, and rain down thunder with devastating efficiency. What they're not supposed to do is shake violently, but that's what happened in January of 2005, just before noon, when one of America's most lethal weapons hit an underwater mountain.

James Akin was the Navy corpsman on board a US Navy submarine when it collided with an undetected rock formation. He remembers how events unfolded over the next two days.

Collision

A few seconds after that initial hit, our sub jolted again and I heard everyone asking if anyone was hurt. Almost immediately the intercom announced there were injured personnel. Multiple injuries. As the corpsman on board, I rushed up to the Combat Systems Equipment Space area of the sub and immediately saw blood everywhere, and two of the sonar technicians had severe head and facial lacerations.

While tending to their injuries, the intercom announced more casualties in the upper-level engine room. I rushed through the passageways and when I got to the engine room, one of the sailors was being helped to the forward compartment. But at the same time I was told about another injured sailor in the Main Sea Water Bay. I found him unconscious and in the fetal position so I called out for my emergency response bag, a stretcher, and a C-collar to secure his neck and spine. He was breathing on his own but it was labored. His eyes were swollen shut and blood was oozing from his nostrils.

By the time the stretcher was brought forward, other shipmates had arrived to assist me with stabilizing him. Once we had him secured on the stretcher, we carried him through the passageways, up a ladder, and into the crew mess room, which had broken dishes and food scattered everywhere due to the violent shaking of the sub. Once there I decided to do triage in the wardroom. With so many injuries, I needed assistance, so I asked Lieutenant JG Litty to run triage, while I worked on the more severe injuries. I directed that all my medical supplies be brought forward and we quickly needed all of the table tops and benches for the wounded, and even the salad bar station was cleared for my supplies.

I concentrated on Machinist Mate Second Class Ashley, who was the most critically injured, using a Propaq to monitor his vitals. I started

The crew of the US Navy submarine *San Francisco* enjoy some well-deserved leisure time while cruising the Pacific. Very soon their travels would take an unexpected and tragic turn. NAVY PHOTO

an intravenous line and gave him oxygen. While checking him out, I was told of another injured sailor from the engine room. He was alert, but hesitated when answering questions, and complained of neck and back pain. As a precaution I put him in a C-collar and placed him on a spine board so we could carry him to the mess room, where I could start an IV and monitor him.

I checked on Petty Officer Ashley, who was on a third and fourth bag of fluids, but I finally got his ins and outs balanced. With assistance from other shipmates, we got Ashley cleaned up but then we started running into issues with the new suction machine and our oxygen supply. We quickly discovered the suction machine would not seal tightly, so we had to jerry rig a new tube and seal it with tape. Just as we solved one problem with the suction machine another one popped up, and I was running out of oxygen and needed to connect Petty Officer Ashley to the ship's oxygen banks.

Directions from Commander Task Force 74, CTF 74, were to use oxygen from the executive officer's stateroom and from the mid-level head (the latrine, for all you non–Navy and Marine types!). But neither of these locations were viable for Petty Officer Ashley, so we had to jerry rig another oxygen source from the crew's mess bleed station. It required an oxygen mask, and as much Tigon tubing as we could find on the sub, secured together with duct tape. To ensure the right amount of oxygen, the bleed line was slowly opened while I felt the oxygen flow until it was at an acceptable rate. More duct tape prevented any leaks and from that point on we had a sufficient supply of oxygen.

Five hours after the incident, I gave Ashley the first dose of mannitol. His vitals were about 200/100, pulse of 140, and respirations of about 52 and shallow. After the mannitol, his vitals came down to about 140/68, pulse around 90, and respiration in the 40s. I was feeling a little more comfortable with his condition, so I wasn't too worried about leaving him while I checked everybody with lacerations, irrigated their wounds, and redressed them properly. Some had deep lacerations that had to be sutured.

After dinner, I gathered up all my sutures, suture kits, and lidocaine. It was already a very long day, and I still had a lot of work to do. A CD player was brought in and the music helped calm down everyone. I was still most concerned about Petty Officer Ashley, who responded favorably to some of his favorite songs. Until this point, someone had to hold the oxygen sensor directly on his hand, and even though he had his arm splinted for the IV, they still had to hold it to keep him from moving around.

This was also about the time we switched communications from CTF 74 to Commander Submarine Pacific Fleet (COMSUBPAC). With so many casualties, I needed guidance from an undersea medical officer to ensure everyone got the treatment and meds they required. But the communication switch resulted in excessive delays and I had to repeat and repeat again vital stats then wait several minutes for instructions. It felt like I was receiving no more help and I was still on my own. I was most concerned about Ashley's facial swelling, but the only guidance I received was to put ice on it, which to me seemed like a very inappropriate comment to be made for the dire situation this sailor was in.

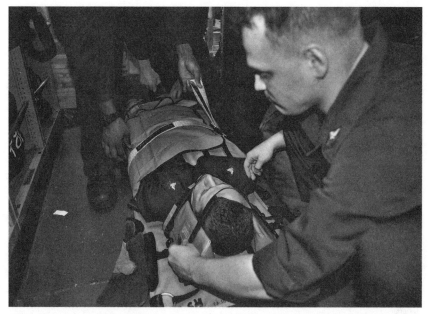

After their sub collided with an undersea mountain, there were numerous injuries. "I found him unconscious and in the fetal position so I called out for . . . a stretcher . . . and a C-collar to secure his neck and spine." NAVY PHOTO

I ended up suturing seven shipmates and finally finished around 2300 hours, though I was interrupted several times to tend to Petty Officer Ashley. I was also given permission to take the second sailor with an injured neck off the backboard, but we left the C-collar on as a precaution.

I returned to Ashley, who remained my priority patient, and I gave him a second dose of mannitol. I was also given direction to administer 5 mg of morphine, though I was hesitant to do that because I was not sure how he was going to react to it, and it was just after midnight before I gave that dose.

Before giving him the morphine, I had everything ready to intubate and ensured that my cricothyrotomy kit was close by. His vital signs had been rising slowly throughout the night. Once I gave the dose of morphine, the vital signs returned to a normal range and his respiration went down to about 40 and was no longer labored.

I felt confident he was out of danger, so Mr. Litty and I agreed to sleep in shifts. I would hit the rack first, with instructions to wake me if my assistance was needed. We had been informed that assistance would be arriving around 0300 hours, but at that same time, Petty Officer Ashley started to take a turn for the worse. The morphine (2.5 mg every hour) was not helping with his vital signs, and we began suctioning his airway.

Around 0330 hours we received word that assistance would not be arriving until possibly sunrise, which was about 0700. It had been a long day and night and we were all exhausted, but we were holding up fine. When I checked on Ashley around 0400, I noticed a massive amount of facial swelling and had to release C-spine precautions to relieve some of the pressure. Forty-five minutes later I received a message from COMSUBPAC to stop administering the mannitol, without knowing exactly why they gave this order. The mannitol, I believed, had been helping, but without it, his vitals were getting worse. By 0700, we found out there was going to be an additional delay, and we did not know when they might arrive.

Finally at 0930, we had additional medical assistance onboard. The first person was a SEAL corpsman, followed by an undersea medical officer from the USS *Cable* who had been a SEAL before going to medical school. The last person down was a search and rescue swimmer. It was quickly determined that Petty Officer Ashley needed to be transferred to the naval hospital at Guam with extreme urgency. A trauma surgeon was mobilized with the medical teams but left on the helicopter to manage him. We wanted to establish an airway before prepping him for the medevac helicopter. We attempted to intubate twice, but both times the critically injured sailor vomited. At that point an incision was required for the airway and the tube was put in, but the cuff on the tube would not hold air so it had to be replaced with another one. This one wouldn't hold air either so a third tube was required. This one held air and was sewn into place.

At this point, we started securing him for the flight outbound. To make it easier to carry the litter up the narrow ladders, handrails were removed and the passageways were cleared. At several points on the sub, such as the ladders, there were several people assisting with the movement of Petty Officer Ashley.

Once he was secured to the stretcher, we started the meandering trip to the command passageway to wait for the medevac helicopter. I led the way through the narrow passageways, which only permitted two people to carry him. At several points, to get him around tight corners, we had to stand him up and during all the jostling, the surgical airway was yanked out. Once we got to the command passageway, the airway was reinserted and sewn back in. Other shipmates were busy rigging the bridge access trunk with a pulley system so we could pull the patient up through the hatch.

Once again though, the airway was yanked out and Ashley had to be lowered back down so we could replace the tube three more times due to faulty cuffs. We finally used a commercial endotracheal tube holder, which is not designed to be used for surgical airways, but miraculously it was a good fit. This time Petty Officer Ashley was hyperventilated before being hoisted up.

Everything was going well during the lift until we reached the bridge access trunk, where the stretcher got stuck. At this point we were all thoroughly frustrated, and reluctantly lowered him back down, again. By this time the medevac helicopter was hovering overhead, and the trauma surgeon was lowered to the boat. He put in a new airway and sewed it in place.

Despite the Mayday call, it took a full day for a medevac chopper to finally arrive the next morning to lower more medical personnel and to fly the injured patient to the naval hospital at Guam. NAVY PHOTO

At this time, Mr. Litty and I dashed back to the crew's mess to get the medical supplies for the trauma surgeon, who reevaluated the patient and could not find a pulse or blood pressure. At that point, CPR was started, and one of our shipmates was doing compressions while another kept bagging to keep oxygen flowing to his lungs. Extreme measures were maintained for thirty minutes, but finally the trauma surgeon pronounced Petty Officer Ashley dead.

Initially I was so numb, overwhelmed, and simply worn out that it didn't hit me that one of my close friends had perished, and just when we were so close to moving him off the sub to a hospital better equipped to take care of him. There was still so much to do and many shipmates to take care of, so I couldn't afford the time to mourn.

(It would be several days later that the loss of Petty Officer Ashley finally hit me, and it was especially hard because he was a friend, and his life was in my hands. Days later the medical examiner determined he had sustained mortal injuries and would have died even if a Level I trauma center was readily available. He was surprised I managed to keep him alive for two days.)

Our deceased shipmate was taken to the wardroom to be cleaned up and placed in the refrigerator until we could arrange his transfer. I briefed the other medical personnel now on board as to the rest of the patients. Once we discussed every patient, I was told to hit the rack. I went to take

Just getting the critically injured shipmate up to the conning tower was a logistical nightmare, trying to maneuver his stretcher down narrow passageways and up tight stairways. Handrails had to be removed and a pulley system jerry-rigged to haul him up to the waiting helicopter. NAVY PHOTO

a shower and change out of my poppie suit, which was soiled with blood, vomit, my own sweat, and other things I don't want to think about.

I tried to lay in my rack, but I couldn't fall asleep. Not after that night from hell. I tried a couple of times before we pulled in but finally gave up. Mr. Litty, who had been with me throughout the chaos, didn't get any sleep either. It would be another twenty-four hours before we pulled in to port. By then, all the patients who needed to go to the ER were identified and prioritized, thirty all told. The most critical were transported by ambulance, the others by medevac buses and vans. As soon as the lines were secured, I went topside to coordinate the transport and treatment of the crew. I was surprised at the numerous medical teams waiting on the pier to assist. They came from the naval hospital at Guam and the USS *Cable* and other ships in port. Once all of our shipmates were on the way to the hospital, I hopped in the last van to catch up with them.

The emergency room was ready to receive all of our patients and had triage set up to handle our numerous injuries. The patients who had broken bones had x-rays and then went to Ortho while other patients remained in the ER. By the end of the night all patients had been seen and three had to be admitted.

—James Akin, Navy Corpsman

(The after-action review of the medical care during this incident resulted in several changes command-wide. Endotrachial tubes were added to the supply system. There was an oxygen regulator made to fit the ship's oxygen system on the crew's mess. Petty Officer Ashley could not fit through the bridge hatch opening while strapped to a stretcher because it would not open to 90 degrees, so modifications were made to ship bridge hatches. There was also fleet training

Navy Corpsman James Akin with Petty Officer Joey Ashley, who succumbed to his injuries after their submarine hit an underwater rock formation. JAMES AKIN PERSONAL PHOTO

implemented. Despite all these changes though, ultimately Navy Corpsman James Akin lost a close friend, a friend he still thinks about today.) Military doctors have to deal with more traumatic injuries in a single deployment to a war zone than most of their civilian counterparts cope with during a lifetime in the ER. Col. Stanley Chartoff was a physician on a critical care air transport team, accompanying wounded warriors on Air Force flights from the war zones of Iraq and Afghanistan to Ramstein Air Base in Germany for surgery at nearby Landstuhl Hospital. During one of these medevac missions, his team was faced with a puzzling case with potentially deadly consequences.

Richard

Richard was an unexpected patient. He wasn't serving in the Area of Responsibility where I was deployed; nor was he one of our typical battle casualties, a victim of the many improvised explosive devices in Afghanistan or a contractor with a critical medical issue. Instead, he was listed as DNBI (Disease Non-Battle Injury) off a ship in the North Atlantic, two continents away. Richard would end up challenging my physical endurance as well as my medical and leadership skills, significantly influencing my professional life, ever after. His mission also provided an unexpected respite during the insanity of war that greatly helped my psyche, if not that of my teammates.

This story actually starts two days before I met Richard, at Bagram Air Base in Afghanistan. It was September 2003, two months into a four-month deployment for Operation Enduring Freedom. This was my second post-9/11 deployment as a critical care physician on a three-man CCATT (critical care air transport team). My civilian specialty is emergency medicine, but the Air Force considers me a critical care doctor. My teammates were Shawn, an emergency room nurse, and Rich, a respiratory therapist, and all of us were from the same Reserve unit stateside, and this was my second CCATT deployment with Shawn in just over a year.

The mission where I would eventually meet Richard started out much like many others I had performed that summer. There were rumors that a Danish soldier was in the Army combat support hospital with a pulmonary embolism, a blood clot in his lung. That rumor was confirmed at the hospital's morning report the next day, so my team assembled our gear to get ready to transport the Dane, who called himself Snoopy, to Landstuhl Army Regional Medical Center in Germany.

A contingent of Marines arrived in Liberia in 2003, but soon developed fevers and respiratory symptoms after working in a warehouse. Some tested positive for malaria, and there was a chance they had come in contact with other deadly viruses in West Africa. NAVY PHOTO

So what's the connection between this patient and Richard? If it were not for Snoopy, our team would not have been in place when circumstances created the opportunity to take the mission where we met Richard.

The seven-hour C-17 flight to Ramstein Air Base was uneventful. An ambulance transported Snoopy and our team on the short ride to Landstuhl. An Air Force ground crew brought us to our hotel, the Hotel American in the city of Ramstein. I had a few beers with the rest of the crew in the lobby, then went to my room, called my wife, and went to bed. It had been twenty-two hours since I had begun my day, in Afghanistan. Two hours after my head hit the pillow, I got a call from the Crew Management Cell, telling us they needed an extra critical care team for a mission to Liberia and we were the only one available. It was 0500 local time. They told me to be ready to be picked up in front of the hotel in thirty minutes. I quickly got dressed, woke up Shawn and Rich, gobbled down food from the hotel's breakfast buffet, and got on the van for the ride back to Ramstein Air Base.

There we learned about a detachment of Marines stationed in Liberia who had developed fever and upper respiratory symptoms after cleaning a warehouse on the docks. Some had tested positive for malaria, but there was concern for leptospirosis and Lassa fever—a deadly and contagious disease of West Africa.

We were told there were fifteen total casualties, seven of those on litters. None of the Marines were on ventilators, but they wanted two critical care teams onsite, just in case. The other team was based at Ramstein, and they needed us because all the other Ramstein teams were stuck at Andrews Air Force Base near Washington, DC. They had gone there on other missions and were waiting for return flights to Germany.

Seven hours after I received the wake up call, the C-17 finally left Germany for an eight-hour flight to Liberia, a typical case of hurry up and wait. It was late afternoon when we landed at the airport in the capital city of Monrovia. It was warm, but not as humid as I expected. This was my first exposure to the African continent. The terminal had a Third World look about it and armed Ravens surrounded the aircraft for security.

The Marines would be arriving from the battleship *Iwo Jima*, which was stationed just off the coast in the North Atlantic Ocean. Soon, three silver Chinook helicopters appeared in the distance, coming closer and landing across the runway from the C-17. A Navy corpsman walked over to give us a report of the casualties, as the Marines were unloaded from the helicopters. It turns out there were actually a total of thirty-one ill Marines, two of them listed as critical.

Carey, the other critical care team doc, and I decided to split the two critical patients and consult on the others, who were assigned to the regular crew, as needed—especially since many of those were on intravenous quinidine, an anti-malaria medication that can affect the heart. My team took the sickest patient, Richard, and Shawn and Rich got him situated on a litter stanchion on the left side of the aircraft.

Richard was a nineteen-year-old lance corporal with brown hair, blue eyes, and a muscular swimmer's build. His patient movement request let

Sick bay on the battleship *Iwo Jima* was overflowing with Marines. Once the critical care air transport team arrived from Germany, thirty-one Marines were transported via Chinook helicopters to the airfield, where the Air Force C-17 was waiting to take them back to Bethesda Hospital, near Washington, DC. MARINE CORPS PHOTO

us know he had been exposed to human and animal feces while cleaning a warehouse three weeks earlier. He had been running fevers as high as 103 degrees for the past two days. He also had diarrhea and was becoming confused. A malaria smear performed on the *Iwo Jima* was positive for falciparum malaria, but there was still the possibility he was infected with leptospirosis and maybe even Lassa fever. He was started on anti-malarial medication and antibiotics, but his condition was worsening.

I first met Richard as the Navy crew brought him onto the rear ramp of the C-17. He had a baby face with a mop of brown hair, cut to Marine standards, and pale, hot, dry skin. His blue eyes were open and he could tell me his name, but not much else. He appeared agitated and was pulling on his intravenous lines, requiring us to place soft cuffs around his wrists as restraints.

We placed an oxygen mask on his face and heart monitor wires on his chest. His heart was racing at 120 beats a minute and his temperature was 102.4 degrees. We did not have time to do much else, as we had to make sure Richard, ourselves, and our equipment were secure for takeoff.

The mission was to deliver the Marines to Bethesda Naval Medical Center, just outside Washington, DC. The first leg was a two-hour flight to Dakar, Senegal, for refueling and to exchange front-end crews. The aircrew had work hour and rest cycle requirements that did not apply to the critical care teams. Richard continued to be agitated, requiring me to order Shawn to administer several doses of Haldol, a sedative.

While Richard was one of the sicker patients I have transported, at least he was whole. Most of the critically injured patients I have taken care of were missing one or more limbs from IED explosions or gunshot wounds. It felt odd not having to deal with that during this mission.

After landing in Dakar, Richard's condition continued to deteriorate. I had not had much experience treating malaria and those I had seen were nowhere near as sick as Richard. These were pre-iPhone days, so I had to rely on the few reference books I brought with me as well as my own medical instinct. I needed more information, and our equipment included a portable blood analyzer. Rich drew a small amount of blood from an artery in Richard's wrist and placed it in the machine. What it showed was that Richard's blood had a critically low level of oxygen and that he was severely anemic. This could have been one of the reasons he was so confused, as not enough oxygen was getting to his brain.

Richard was already on the maximum amount of oxygen he could get from a mask, so I decided he needed to be placed on a ventilator. My team assembled the medications and equipment we needed to place a tube into his trachea. However, this was the first time I had performed this procedure on a real patient on a C-17 and I learned a valuable lesson. We had a litter in the upper position of the stanchion over Richard to hold equipment. What I found out is I could not get the proper line of vision with that litter in place to pass the tube down his throat. I kept my cool, however, and we got other crew members to move the litter while I stayed in position and passed the tube. Mission success! That need for situational awareness is something that has stayed with me ever since.

My team was finishing with getting Richard stabilized when I heard a commotion on the other side of the cabin. One of the Marines in the noncritical group had suddenly become unresponsive. He was breathing okay, but was not responding even to pain. Carey, whose other patient was very stable, took charge and set him up to be intubated as well. He almost had the same mishap I did, but I coached him along, knowing he was a cardiologist and hadn't done this procedure very often.

Now we still had to address Richard's other problem, which was severe anemia. He needed a blood transfusion, and it couldn't wait till we landed stateside. I had no idea where I was going to find suitable blood in Dakar, and we only had about an hour left before we had to take off again. At this point, a young man in a Hawaiian shirt spoke up and said, "I can get you some blood."

I had my doubts, but he identified himself as an Air Force flight surgeon assigned to the Liberian embassy in Monrovia. Because of heightened threats, he was relocated to Dakar and was staying in the local Club

Thirty-one Marines had gotten sick while deployed to Liberia, and two of those were listed as critical. Once loaded and secured on the C-17 transport flight, they would be flown to the DC area for treatment at Bethesda. AIR FORCE PHOTO

Med. He knew of a Navy ship at the port of Dakar that had a blood bank. He worked some magic and was able to get us two units of blood cells. The way total strangers can use trust and ingenuity and work together in foreign surroundings as a team and accomplish great things resounds with me to this day.

We took off from Dakar for the final eight-hour leg to Andrews Air Force Base. Richard kept my team busy for most of the trip. I needed to put a special catheter in the artery in his wrist to closely monitor his blood pressure and allow us to draw blood for testing. Shawn, Rich, and I worked together to keep him sedated, keep his blood pressure under control, and adjust his ventilator to maximize the oxygen getting to his brain and the rest of his body. We continued to treat the malaria and other infections. My hope was that his body and especially his brain were resilient enough to fully recover their normal functions. I looked at this nineteen-year-old baby-faced Marine and realized he was just starting his life and had so much to look forward to when he got home. I wondered if, like most of the Marines I have met, that as soon as he was well enough, he would want to go right back to the fight.

Somewhere over the Atlantic, Rich glanced at Richard's monitor and noticed the oxygen reading was dropping down. As any good respiratory therapist would, Rich checked his equipment and discovered the ventilator was no longer functioning. Quickly, he disconnected him and started ventilating him manually with a bag connected to oxygen. Richard's oxygen levels improved. Looking at the ventilator, we were able to determine that a fuse was blown, but the alarm indicator was difficult to see and if there was an alarm, you could not hear it above the din of the plane. With this fuse out, the power cord did not function, so when the battery charge wore down, the machine stopped. (This same problem would happen to us again on a later mission, prompting a notification up the chain, resulting in changes by the manufacturer and the availability of spare fuses.)

As we neared Andrews, I noticed that one of the Marines whom I had seen walking around earlier in the flight was now lying down with a high-flow oxygen mask on. I asked one of the nurses about him and was told he became confused and his oxygen levels on the monitor dropped when he took the mask off. He was breathing fast even with the mask on.

I asked Rich to check his blood oxygen and it was adequate, and since we were close to landing, I decided to just keep a close eye on him and bring him with us to the ICU at Bethesda. I found out later he ended up being the sickest Marine on the plane.

Richard finally stabilized as we began our descent into Andrews. We landed and the ramp on the back of the C-17 was opened and a medical team from Bethesda came on board to meet us. When they did, our initial response was silence and nervous looks at each other because the Bethesda team was wearing protective gowns, hats, and gloves while we stood there in our flight suits.

They gave us no explanation at the time, but I later learned after a heated discussion with one of the chief flight surgeons that the medical authority at Bethesda decided not to inform the receiving team that malaria was identified as the infectious agent, and therefore not contagious. They wanted the team to exercise treating an unknown infectious disease and test their isolation procedures. I wish someone had told us it was just an exercise. Maybe our pucker level wouldn't have spiked when we first saw them all suited up.

Richard and the other three critical Marines were moved to a bus specially equipped for critical care transfers as we prepared for the forty-five-minute trip around the Washington Beltway to Bethesda. Richard decided he wasn't ready to let us relax, so he dropped his oxygen levels again, requiring us to manually bag him on oxygen. We also noted that his blood pressure was precipitously dropping. We told the bus driver to drive with lights and sirens as we tried to stabilize Richard. Shawn showed great skill as he prepared a drip of medication as the bus careened

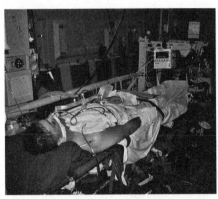

Richard was a nineteen-year-old Marine corporal who became gravely ill in Liberia. He had numerous symptoms, but there were no definitive answers to what was slowly but deliberately taking his life.
AIR FORCE PHOTO

past the notoriously bad Washington-area drivers. As Shawn finished setting the drip up, I knelt down and noticed fluid dripping on the floor. There had been a leak in the pressure monitor line, giving us the abnormal values. Well at least we had learned how well we could perform on a moving bus.

The bus arrived at the Navy Medical Center and the two critical care teams accompanied the four Marines to the ICU. Richard was settled in his room, a welcome change from the back of a C-17, and Shawn, Rich, and I each gave status reports to our counterparts at Bethesda, and readied our equipment to return to Andrews. Richard was in very capable hands.

I could end this story here, but as a result of this unexpected mission with Richard, what happened next did so much to elevate my psyche and make the last two months of deployment bearable for the three of us, or at least I thought so at the time. Standing in the lobby of the Medical Center, I realized I was in the States again and could make an easy phone call home without dealing with overseas operators. Then we learned it was Sunday and our return flight wasn't until Tuesday. The three of us did the math and realized we were six hours from home and it was worth the effort. We tried Union Station in DC first, but there were no trains to our destination. Instead we rented a car, arriving home at 0230. I hugged my very surprised and sleepy but happy wife and kids, then slept until morning. I had a great full day with my family, but saying goodbye again was the hardest part. Always is. Shawn and Rich reported similar experiences with their loved ones, and despite heavy traffic in Baltimore, we made it back to Andrews with plenty of time to spare as our return plane trip was delayed.

If it weren't for our mission with Richard, I would have never had the chance to go home in the middle of a war. I was recharged and the rest of the deployment was less stressful knowing that I could look forward to returning home again. This same strength supported me during the next deployment and anytime I needed to be away from home for a prolonged period of time.

So what happened to Richard? I never did get to meet this strong young Marine in a state of wellness, but I learned from the doctors at Bethesda that he had suffered what is known as cerebral malaria, where

After the C-17 medical transport plane arrived at Andrews Air Base, a medical team dressed in protective gear came aboard to load up the four critically ill patients for the forty-five-minute drive to Bethesda Hospital. AIR FORCE PHOTO

the malaria organisms clog up the arteries to the brain causing strokes and coma. Carey's Marine had the same outcome. Within days of arriving at Bethesda, Richard was awake and able to be taken off the ventilator. Unfortunately, his respiratory status worsened as he developed a condition called ARDS. He needed to be placed back on the ventilator for a period of days, but eventually improved and had a full recovery. I later learned that the reason these Marines developed malaria was they had not been taking their malaria prevention pills. They were prescribed mefloquine, which has known significant side effects. Also most were not using insect repellent and none were using bed netting.

Richard inadvertently became a poster child for how easily and cheaply malaria can be controlled with adherence to proper precautions, and how severely it can cripple our fighting force. He was not only the one patient who has helped me become a better doctor, teammate, airman, husband, and father, but he showed the military how its response to those Disease Non-Battle Injury patients can greatly influence the protection and strength of our men and women in uniform.

—Col. Stanley E. Chartoff, US Air Force Reserves

While Iraq and Afghanistan have dominated the nightly news cycles during the past decade, there have been numerous other regional skirmishes and conflicts, some of which the average American would not be able to pinpoint on a world map. Sarajevo, Mogadishu, and Kosovo are just a few of these soon-forgotten war zones, but on occasion American military forces are called on to provide humanitarian assistance, to quell high seas piracy, or even to save a little boy.

Mission to Kosovo and Back

In the summer of 1999, it was early in the evening when the call came
forth that approval had been obtained and orders were cut for our critical care air transport team to fly to Kosovo and fly a ten-year-old Albanian boy from there to Landstuhl Regional Medical Center, LRMC, in
Germany. As part of the Kosovo Force (KFOR), a US Army medical
team had been caring for the boy after he sustained significant internal
trauma from a crush injury outside the complex when a concrete pillar fell on his abdomen. He was rushed to surgery within the KFOR
medical unit, then over the next four to five days, his course was complicated by the development of a necrotizing fasciitis. Under the care of a
US Army internist there, he appeared to be improving. Still, significant
skin grafting following the necrotizing fasciitis was required, and NATO
determined the boy should be moved to a German facility specializing
in such procedures.

At the time, the only American facility with a neonatal intensive care
unit (NICU) in the European Theater was Landstuhl, operated by a joint
assignment of US Air Force and Army neonatal personnel. Based out of
this NICU was a neonatal critical care air transport team (NCCATT),
which is why we were tasked with flying to Kosovo to care for the boy
during the flight back to Germany. As the neonatologist on-call that evening, the mission fell to me to organize and conduct the transport. I made
the decision to take not only a neonatal intensive care unit nurse, Deb, but
also one of the adult intensive care nurses, Matt. Fortunately our respiratory therapist, Chris, was well trained in the care of patients from infants
to the elderly.

When we huddled to begin planning the mission, we made the decision to bring the adult CCATT bags, a set of Breslow bags, and equipment

as appropriate for a ten-year-old boy of average size. We also added to the pharmacy bag medications routinely used in the pediatric ICU. There was not a set pediatric CCATT with allocated equipment and supplies at Landstuhl or nearby Ramstein Air Base.

Once prepared, the ambulance transported us off the hill from Landstuhl to Ramstein and the C-9 Nightingale transport plane that awaited us. Fortunately it was a very nice German summer night and no storms were in the forecast. When we arrived on the C-9, we were met by the 86th Aeromedical Evacuation Squadron team, and we quickly compared notes on the mission ahead. Each member had a significant part to play in the success of the mission, and together we formed quite the team. As with every mission, to ensure its success, communication was vital.

What happened next will always remain imprinted in my

It was a humanitarian mission to Kosovo, flying in to pick up an Albanian boy who had been crushed when a concrete pillar fell on him. "This was the very first time in my career I had a pre-flight briefing dedicated solely to discussing the hostile threat of snipers in the area of operation we were flying into." AIR FORCE PHOTO

mind. I have personally completed now over 140 air and ground transport missions, to include international, transatlantic, trans-Pacific, and missions within the United States. I have worked in numerous aircraft from the large C-5 to the small US Coast Guard Falcon. Nothing fazed me with regard to the mission at hand, and adapting to each circumstance and environment was part of the process. Still, this was the very first time in my career I had a pre-flight briefing dedicated solely to discussing the hostile threat of snipers in the area of operation we were flying into. I am sure this part of the job becomes routine after a while for those men and women in service deployed to hostile environments, but I am equally sure, just as with me, their first briefing is always the most memorable. Any time after that, we have been reminded of how human we are and the risks we take on each mission, as we try to save a life. We never even think that we might lose another in the process, much less that it could be one of our own.

We departed Ramstein and headed south. After several hours, we began to turn toward Albania. The pilot had us pull the shades down on all the windows. The pre-briefing had discussed snipers lurking in the fields surrounding the airport we were going to be landing at. Even though our plane clearly displayed a large red cross on the sides, it would seem more like a giant bull's eye to those enemy snipers. As a further precaution, the lighting in the cabin was dimmed. Understandably a sense of urgency and danger increased as the sun began to rise, and we landed in Kosovo. I quickly realized it was a bright sunny day outside and any snipers had an unobstructed view of our arrival.

Once on the ground, we waited for the Black Hawk helicopter carrying the boy, his parents, and the Army internist to arrive from the KFOR hospital. This internist had been the sole caregiver for this boy since his surgery, forming a strong bond with his family and caring for the boy as though he was his own. The Black Hawk touched down not far from where we were parked on the flight line, but even that short distance was exposed to any snipers watching.

A contingency of ground troops wearing body armor came to our plane and surrounded it, watching over both us and the helicopter, but they never came into view until I saw them escort the litter team from the Black Hawk to the C-9 ramp. Of course, our pilot and his crew had 9mm Berettas in shoulder harnesses in plain view, and the team that carried the boy on board had shouldered their M-16 rifles until we had secured the stretcher into the C-9, which had a large door along the front left side where an opening formed a ramp to the ground. That's when I first felt any sense of real danger . . . when those big doors of the aircraft opened up to welcome in the outside world. I remember peering around the side of the doorway, protected by the fuselage, looking at the surrounding fields, wondering if a sniper was looking at our little operation and waiting to send a round our way.

From our briefing prior to leaving Landstuhl, we had gotten a report that the boy was improving, but "improving" is hardly how I would describe the lifeless little boy we were tasked with saving. Upon first glance, I saw a small person about four feet tall stretched out on a green Army litter with enough lines coming off and equipment attached to catch radio frequencies for miles. His belly was filleted open, exposing raw flesh similar to what you'd see in a butcher's shop. He had two pieces of tubing coming from somewhere underneath the flesh attached to two plastic grenade drains, filled with a red-tinged yellow fluid. His chest was exposed and heaved with each breath of the ventilator. His face was obscured from the endotracheal tube and tape that held his life support in place.

A Black Hawk helicopter carried the injured boy, his parents, and an Army internist who had been his sole caregiver since his surgery. Snipers were lurking in the nearby hills and fields around Rinas Airport in Albania. After the Black Hawk touched down, a contingent of local ground troops surrounded the passengers and escorted them the short distance to the waiting transport plane.
AIR FORCE PHOTO

Still, as I looked closer, I began to make out his sandy, brown disheveled hair. Gradually, the raw flesh disappeared and upon the arrival of his mother at the bedside, the young boy emerged, an innocent victim of another one of man's senseless conflicts.

He could have been the boy playing baseball in our German neighborhood the day before, or the child photographed in the *Stars and Stripes* for the large fish he caught over the weekend. He could also have been the son of any one of us. No matter, when it comes to CCATT teams, our patients become family and we treat each as though they were our own. It's sort of an unspoken code for CCATT members.

He had already undergone a successful debridement from the necrotizing fasciitis. When he came on board, he was on a broad spectrum of antibiotics, and was getting good pain control, but there was very little movement, and that was an ominous sign. He was also on a ventilator, but at relatively low settings. As we settled in and got the boy on our monitors, Deb and Matt turned to me with the first set of vitals. The boy's heart rate was in the 160s, his temperature was 103.2 degrees Fahrenheit, and he was hypotensive. We knew then, this was not going to be a routine CCATT transport, but then again, that's why we carry the supplies and equipment we do. Stabilized patients can become unstable at any time in the transport. By bringing the ICU supplies, equipment, and team expertise to the patient, the intensive care can begin before their arrival. This C-9 became our ICU for the next twelve hours.

Once airborne, and away from the dangers of Kosovo airspace, we began to work steadily. We started with fluid boluses, began pressor drips with dopamine and dobutamine, eventually using epinephrine, and placed an arterial line. We drew repeated blood cultures and switched his antibiotics to more powerful, broad-spectrum drugs. Still, we lacked any antifungals in our bag, and we knew this was probably the underlying culprit for this child's acute deterioration. Laboratory tests on our i-Stat portable machine disclosed the boy was hypoglycemic and acidotic from both a metabolic and respiratory component. The internist stated the boy had begun to feel warm as they boarded the Black Hawk. In addition, they had noted a drop in urine output over the past few hours. What we were facing was a septic child in multi-organ failure.

During the entire flight, which was well over twelve hours, the parents watched our every move. On very rare occasions did I notice one of them resting in a seat, while the other stood vigil. I often wondered how scared they must have been, sitting in a plane with their child obviously very sick, listening to the team work but not understanding a single spoken word, and not being able to gain the comfort one gets and needs by hearing those words from the medical team, "It's going to be all right."

While at Landstuhl, on numerous occasions, we had used the pediatric ICU in Homberg, a town in Saarland, just about twenty minutes down the road. They had a well-respected pediatric intensive care unit as well as pediatric surgery and other important pediatric sub-specialties.

Once the critically injured Albanian boy and his parents were loaded on board, the neonatal critical care air transport team was tasked with stabilizing him for the trip to Ramstein Air Base in Germany, where he would get the life-saving care he needed at a German hospital. AIR FORCE PHOTO

As the plane was refueling in Aviano, I called the Homberg PICU and described the situation. Without hesitation, they accepted the case, realizing the urgency and critical nature of the boy's condition. There was no time to wait for NATO approval of the switch, nor would it be necessary, for as I later found out, when it comes to kids, everyone in the chain of command is sympathetic and understanding.

When we arrived at Ramstein, folks at Landstuhl and the air base had already sprung into action. The ambulance was kept running on the flight line, waiting for our arrival. Once secured, it quickly took us to Homberg. The boy's blood pressure was hanging in there at low normal. His cap refill was two to three seconds, he was producing some urine, and after significant changes on the ventilator, had a normal CO_2. Still, he was on 75 percent oxygen and we were certain he had evolving acute respiratory distress syndrome from the sepsis. It seemed like an hour or more, but we finally arrived at Homberg, and they quickly took over the care of this boy hanging on to life.

In the days that followed, we learned the offending micro-organism was *Candida*. In addition, it took several days of intensive care before the boy was in the clear, and several weeks before he was eventually transported to the German skin unit. He received successful skin grafting and three months after the transport flight, he returned to Kosovo with his family. Looking back, though I never did a lot of talking with the family that trip, primarily because they did not speak English and we had no interpreter on the plane. I did notice they seemed to key in on our actions and expressions quite a lot during the transport. So as a team, we did our most to always look reassuring, knowing there was no certainty the boy would survive.

Later, the *Stars and Stripes* would write a story on the internist and the boy, briefly mentioning the use of a specialized transport team to move the child out of Kosovo. Chris came to me with the article and at first seemed disgruntled that we were not mentioned or even interviewed for the piece. I asked him if that would really change the feeling he had inside for the life we saved and the gratitude the family expressed to each of us as they hugged us at the end of the transport. Quickly, he grinned and put the paper down.

Lt. Col. Robert Holcomb: "I quickly realized, looking back, that war knows no boundaries. An innocent boy, playing in the rubble of a bombed-out city, falls victim to the unstable foundation that once held his life together. The pillar came crashing down on him, and his life would never be the same. I had taken care of so many children who were sick or had been involved in trauma such as motor vehicle accidents, but I had never before cared for a war victim." ROBERT HOLCOMB PERSONAL PHOTO

I am forever proud of that transport and my colleagues: Chris, Deb, Matt, the 86th AES, and the crew of that C-9 Nightingale. Just like the men and women of the service today, they are a major part of what makes this nation strong. I saw excellence in each and every one of them that day and discovered a true sense of self-worth in myself as well.

I quickly realized, looking back, that war knows no boundaries. An innocent boy, playing in the rubble of a bombed-out city, falls victim to the unstable foundation that once held his life together. The pillar came crashing down on him, and his life would never be the same. I had taken care of so many children who were sick or had been involved in trauma such as motor vehicle accidents, but I had never before cared for a war victim.

Battlefield injuries were supposed to be reserved for the soldiers and Marines on the battlefield, the airmen in the skies, the sailors on the seas. Sure, I had seen pictures on TV, read stories in the paper, viewed Hollywood movies at the theater. These proved to be nothing but a short trailer to the real film being made that night in that C-9 Nightingale.

God put me on this earth for a purpose, and that day exemplified more than any what that purpose was.

—Lt. Col. Robert G. Holcomb, Air Force Neonatologist

The business of preparing for war often requires dangerous training exercises that leave the participants vulnerable to injuries or worse. Sometimes someone makes a crucial mistake that ends up having severe consequences. And sometimes high-tech equipment simply breaks down.

Ditched at Sea

Working in a naval hospital, even one of the Navy's "big three," there's just not that many trauma patients. We certainly have quite a few wounded warriors going through rehab and follow-up surgeries, but with several major trauma centers in the area, emergency patients typically go to one of those first, regardless of if they are military or not.

Trauma is what I love, and since becoming an RN, I've worked in both Level I and Level II trauma centers. When I decided to become a nurse, I wanted to be where the best hospitals were, so after I graduated from nursing school and got my RN I was commissioned in the Navy. Here we work rotating shifts of two months of days, then two months of nights, plus every other weekend, with no end. We see all kinds of patients, from coughs and colds to heart attacks.

First-time parents—and there are a lot of them in the military—get really nervous when their child gets fussy and feels warm, so they bring them straight in. Most patients don't try to get an appointment with their primary care doctor and just come to the ER instead. We might get someone who's had a cough for the past seven weeks, or a headache, or a toothache.

Our average was three hundred patients per day with about fifteen admissions, and those were the ones who were really sick. Don't get me wrong, we would get a lot of lacerations that needed stitches, or the occasional heart attacks or strokes. As such, we were a very busy ER, with fourteen thousand visits annually, and there was usually no time to rest in-between patients. Just like in civilian emergency rooms, most people could not get in to see their primary care physician quickly, so we saw everyone!

I'm a bit obsessive-compulsive—most ER nurses are—and I find great satisfaction in taking something that is chaos and turning it into

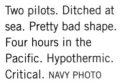
Two pilots. Ditched at sea. Pretty bad shape. Four hours in the Pacific. Hypothermic. Critical. NAVY PHOTO

order and fixing it. I'd probably enjoy restoring an old car for the same reason. I am good at multitasking and prioritizing. In the ER there are so many things to be accomplished, and decisions are made based on what is the most important or urgent. Then get that done first, then on to the next priority. Some nurses just can't hang in the ER. Burnout is a huge issue with all nursing. We work twelve-hour shifts (or longer), and we work two days on then two days off. Then we work three days on with two days off. Nurses who can't hang can't handle the fact there's never enough time to get everything done, or they can't handle the pressure of all of the things happening all at once. In nursing, multitasking is essential to survival. Certainly we also get stuck in the mundane, but unlike a civilian emergency room, we get to work a lot with wounded warriors, and that is very rewarding.

This one particular night, we were pretty busy. We got a call saying a helicopter would be bringing us two pilots who had ditched over water. That first phone call seemed like it was no big deal, and if they were coming to us they obviously couldn't be trauma patients. We made preparations anyway and moved patients out of our larger rooms so we would have room to work, and so these two pilots could be close together and we could focus our resources.

Several hours later we got another call explaining both pilots were pretty bad off and very hypothermic after they had spent over four hours in the Pacific Ocean. When the plane developed mechanical problems, the navigator had punched out, while the pilot had stayed with the plane, attempting to save it, so when it finally crashed at sea, the two aviators were separated by several miles, making it difficult for the recovery team to locate both of them.

The helicopter that was transporting them was too big to land at any local trauma center, so they were headed our way. The pucker factor went up. We gave Orthopedics and the operating room a heads up, then prepared for the worst.

The pilots, both from Miramar Air Station, arrived still in their flight suits, soaked in jet fuel and hurting real bad. One pilot, whom I will call Joker, had two broken arms and an open fracture to his femur. We couldn't even take his blood pressure due to his fractures. The challenge with a trauma patient is to determine what to do first, and most of the time, things are done simultaneously. The pilot's core temperature was so low it wouldn't register on the thermometer.

I told him we were going to have to take a rectal temperature, and as I was rolling him on his side he jokingly asked me if I was going to buy him a drink first.

To me this exemplifies the spirit of every military member. Even when we are broken, even when we don't know if we are going to live, we're still in good humor, and we still choose to live.

The second pilot, whom I'll call Maverick, wasn't as bad. He was hypothermic as well but had no fractures. It was a very

When their plane developed mechanical troubles over the Pacific, the two pilots from Miramar Air Station punched out, but they were separated by several miles, making it difficult for the rescue crew to locate them. NAVY PHOTO

tense couple of hours working on both pilots, warming their cores, splinting fractures, and preparing Joker for surgery. Due to their severe hypothermia we had to warm them with warm saline through IVs and with warming blankets. They asked for hot chocolate or coffee, but we never give trauma patients anything by mouth—this is called NPO (nothing post-oral)—because they will probably be going to the operating room and they could not go under anesthesia if they'd had anything to eat or drink within several hours. The NPO precaution decreases the risk of aspirating during the surgery.

The pilots had spent a long time in the freezing water; Joker had compound fractures and the search helicopter had noticed sharks circling nearby, though the two pilots never saw them. When they first landed, Joker couldn't deploy his life vest, and he sank below the surface of the water, but luckily his vest auto-inflated, thus saving his life. (A life raft is not part of their survival gear. They have on survival vests that auto-inflate if they go below so many feet in the water. They have a whistle and a pen flare, which don't do much good unless they see a rescue boat or plane. It certainly doesn't do anything to ward off any sharks!)

Both of these pilots were very lucky to survive their experience, but they lived, thanks to their amazing resilience and attitudes.

With two broken arms and femur, the pilot could not support himself on the rescue sling, so he had to be strapped to a stretcher before he could be lifted to the Coast Guard plane overhead. NAVY PHOTO

These two patients reminded me of some car accident victims I had treated at VCU Trauma Center in Richmond, Virginia. There were many things to do all at once, and there was a lot of pressure because they could die if we didn't do things right. They were really cold and dehydrated and we had to start large IVs on them. We had to get them warm and get x-rays and stabilize fractures and give them pain medications.

In the ER, it can get a little hectic at times. As a nurse, the doctors are always shouting out orders, and there is a point when you already know what needs to be done. There are also times when you might "suggest" things to the doctor, and then they say, "Yeah that's a good idea."

At a teaching hospital when you have residents it is a whole other challenge. They sometimes give bad or dangerous orders. As a nurse with years of experience, you can either tell them they are stupid or try to guide them to the right conclusion. The latter is obviously the better option, because then you don't make an enemy, and also they develop into a better doctor in the end!

We didn't have those issues. Our team pulled together, and we did our job and saved those two pilots' lives. We were able to mobilize all of our resources and do what we normally didn't do and take care of two trauma patients at once without hesitation! I wish I could say both of these aviators returned to duty, but unfortunately, the pilot had to leave the service due to his injuries, and the navigator eventually returned home, to civilian life.

To this day, I enjoy being a trauma nurse. Certainly it is challenging, but it's also very rewarding.

—Carl Hill, ER/Trauma Nurse

Sometimes simple acts of kindness have enormous impacts on those we've touched. For Navy Corpsman Jason Unruh, it happened during a humanitarian mission to war-torn Somalia while treating local villagers.

Jambo

They knew we were there. More than two thousand desperate villagers from around Witu in Kenya had arrived seeking medical care. Some had walked for miles. Some had never seen a doctor before and definitely required attention. It was exhausting, rewarding, sometimes even a little intimidating to see so many in so little time, as we bounced from one patient to the next for hours on end. I never would have imagined it, that I would come so far, looking back on where this all started for me. . . .

Finishing high school at the bottom of my class, I had zero college prospects and no real idea what I wanted to do for a living. I'd had a job of one form or another since I was thirteen, and finding work was never really an issue. I had worked for about a year as an orderly at the nearby hospital and started taking classes at the local technical college, but my head really wasn't in the game. In a rather impulsive move I joined the Navy—"see the world"—picking hospital corpsman as my occupational specialty, because according to the recruiter, it was pretty much doing the same as the orderly job I had at the time.

Well, like all recruiters he didn't really lie, he just neglected to mention a few things I might need to know to make an informed decision. Two years later I found myself attached to the 2nd Battalion, 5th Marines, in a floating metal box known as the USS *Peleliu*, off the war-torn coast of Somalia.

Life attached with the Marines on an amphibious assault ship, looking out at the vast nothingness of blue water and distant coastline, as we did grid squares, known as modified location, is tedious and cramped, and to say I was going stir crazy would be an understatement. When any opportunity to get off that ship came up I jumped at it, not really caring what I was going to be doing but just wanting off the ship.

The Marine Corps—much to the dismay of the Corps—is part of the Navy, and receives all of its medical support from Navy doctors and corpsmen. I was one of the latter. Navy corpsmen assigned to the Fleet Marine Force (FMF) are detailed to one of the three Marine divisions and assigned to individual battalions from there.

Each Marine infantry battalion has a battalion aid station or BAS, usually headed up by a young Navy doctor fresh out of internship, who fills the role of the battalion surgeon. Also assigned to the aid station is an independent duty corpsman (IDC) on the medical side and a chief hospital corpsman for everything else. The life of a corpsman with the Fleet Marines is dramatically different than it is in the hospital or onboard a ship.

My recruiter had been right about my Navy corpsman job being the same in the hospital as in the civilian facility where I worked as an orderly. It involved providing the basics of care, such as making sure patients had water, that IVs were still flowing, helping folks in and out of bed, taking their vital signs, changing bedpans, and running records. The doctors and nurses performed all of the skilled tasks, such as ordering and administering medications, and any medical or surgical procedures.

Duty with the Marines was a completely different role. Corpsmen do it all. The fresh young doctor finds himself responsible for the care of around eleven hundred Marines and sailors. As a corpsman, I spent most of my time with the Marines, and my duties were all encompassing, requiring the Marines to have absolute faith in me, even if it was completely unfounded. Like it or not, you tend to get close to people you have to "puppy pile" with in the field to keep from freezing at night.

And even if we really don't know everything about everything, the Marines we work with every day think we do. I actually had a Marine one time whose wife had migraines. After her visit to the neurologist, she came home with a long list of diet restrictions and activities to avoid. Her husband came up to me and said, "The doctor told my wife she can't eat chocolate and needed to drink more coffee when she felt a headache coming on. Does that sound right to you Doc, or is he full of shit?"

Of course I assured him the neurologist had about fifteen years of training and education and probably knew what he was talking about, but this Marine needed my validation, because when you're a grunt you have a hard time trusting anyone else, especially someone you don't know.

For the corpsman there are three ways to deal with this kind of responsibility. You can stay within your training and pass off things you can't handle. You can fake it and hope you don't kill anybody, or you can spend every spare minute of free time poring through whatever medical books you can find—beg, borrow, buy, or steal—and pester your doctor to death with "what if . . . ?" questions, trying to learn as much as you can before you really need it, because it's always when you are as far away as possible from the next level of care that shit goes sideways and you are ultimately and solely responsible for your Marines.

All three options are dangerous, though I'd like to think I was in the last category, studying as much as possible whenever and wherever I could. But early on there was still a lot of well-intentioned, semi-educated guessing going on, and to be completely honest, that part of urgent care in the field has never really changed, which in a really roundabout way takes us back to sitting off the coast of Africa in a huge metal box.

The opportunity I spoke of to get off that ship was known as a MED-CAP, or Medical Civilian Assistance Program, visit to Witu in Kenya, a small coastal village north of Mombasa. Due to shallow reefs and the lack of a suitable landing zone for the helicopters, we used inflatable landing craft from the ship, but the only suitable beach to land on in the dense junglelike forest was about three miles from the village.

We had taken ashore a few vehicles, but they were loaded down with supplies so most of us hiked in to the village on a narrow dirt road. Along the way we passed a number of local homes, most of them nothing more than a collection of twigs and vines woven into loose walls that were then packed with grass and mud to form a type of adobe hut.

Most of the roofs were constructed of thatched palm fronds, but several were formed out of a patchwork of discarded plastic sheets and old ragged tarps. Meals were being cooked over small open fires. Each home had a small garden plot next to it with a low bramble fence marking the borders of the homestead.

The village itself had a few more permanent structures of cut wood, cinder blocks, stucco, and plaster. The largest building in town was the

"Some had never seen a doctor before." The medical team had hundreds of villagers, ranging from newborns to the elderly, waiting for them. NAVY PHOTO

clinic, a single-story block and stucco structure on a raised foundation, roughly one hundred feet long by forty feet wide. We were told it was the only building in town that had running water and electricity. The windows were screened without glass, using shutters instead during bad weather.

On the first day of our humanitarian mission, we saw somewhere in the neighborhood of twenty-five hundred people, far exceeding our expectations. Some of the people had walked four to five hours to see the "American doctors." To the majority who came to us, it didn't matter that most of us weren't actually doctors. We listened to their complaints through broken English and the aid of our local translators and treated them the best we could with the supplies we brought. To say the local clinic was understocked would be overstating its capabilities. Two to three bottles of quinine for malaria and a few old muslin bandages left over from some forgotten war were the best to be had prior to our arrival.

Two distinct events stand out from our first day in Witu. A middle-aged man had injured his left hand with a machete, and now the wound was a week or so old and the infection had spread so extensively that by the time we finished debriding the necrotic tissue, you could see through his hand between his ring and middle fingers. Our independent duty corpsman thought it should be amputated, but we did not have the drugs or the supplies to do the job. He tanked him up instead on every brand of antibiotic we had and hoped somehow he was tough enough to beat the infection. He was at a very high risk for gangrene and sepsis, but it was the best we could do.

The second event involved the clinic's nurse. The only person to regularly work out of that clinic, she was a traveling nurse who spent one day each week in Witu, and returned with the local doctor on his monthly visit. As often as possible we relied on injections for any medications we administered. We were told that any pills or "take home" medications would either be sold to or stolen by Somali fighters who frequently raided the area. I had just finished giving a man a shot of antibiotics for an infection and went to drop the syringe in the industrial-size disposal I had placed next to the bed I was working from, but the trash bin was gone.

A quick survey of the room revealed that all the waste containers were gone. I managed to find them all in the clinic kitchen. Turns out the nurse had collected them up and had pried the lids off them, which was no easy feat, and she was disassembling the needles and syringes and putting

Navy Corpsman Jason Unruh spent two days in the village of Witu, Kenya, seeing more than three thousand patients. JASON UNRUH PERSONAL PHOTO

them in pots of boiling water to clean and sterilize them for reuse. She was very upset when I told her the syringes and needles were single use only and must be thrown away.

However she was very happy to learn we planned on leaving about a thousand needles and syringes with her when we left.

(When we were leaving Camp Pendleton weeks earlier, we had spoken with the people at the medical supply warehouse and arranged to dispose of all of their soon-to-expire medical supplies. I can't remember everything we got, but I did manage to salvage close to a thousand doses of Ceftriaxone, a high-powered antibiotic, eight hundred bags of IV fluid, and about five thousand needle and syringe combos. At that time the medical supplies had to be destroyed six months out from the expiration date. Nowadays we can swap unused supplies with the vendors, but back then we would throw out tons of stuff every year.)

The rest of the day in Witu was tiring, but uneventful, with most patients being treated for schistosomiasis or malaria. We left at three o'clock for our long walk back to the beach, followed by a long ride back to the ship. I was very surprised when, at 0430 the next morning, I was being awoken to go back to Witu. I was not scheduled to go on the second day, to allow everyone a chance to get off the ship if they wanted. Either by mistake or fate, I found myself repeating my trek of the previous day.

The second day at Witu was busier than the first, and by the time it was said and done over thirty-one hundred men, women, and children had passed through our little makeshift clinic. About mid-morning I noticed an excited man at the door waving at me and gesturing in my direction. I vaguely recognized him from the day before as one of the patients I had treated.

Before I could put things together, he got his message across to the doorkeeper and he was headed my way. From behind his back he pulled two shy young girls about ages six and seven, one in each hand. Before I could say "Jambo" (hello in Swahili), the two girls ran up, each grabbing one of my hands and promptly kissing them. The father was talking about a mile a minute to the translator, who was struggling to keep up with his broken English. In the end it came down to this: The father had walked ten kilometers and had waited four hours to be seen by me the day before and was so happy with his care that he wanted his daughters to be seen by the same American "doctor." The girls both had schistosomiasis, which we quickly treated. I was thanked again profusely by all three and eventually they left so I could attend to the next patient brought in.

That was twenty-three years ago. I continued on in the Navy, going to IDC School, and on to become a Navy physician assistant. Today I find myself as the battalion surgeon for a Marine Corps "grunt" battalion. I have seen many things since that first of eight deployments and treated countless patients, but it's those two little girls and their father who stand out in my memory. Collectively they are "The One" who affirmed my calling to a life of service in medicine. They are the patients who keep me going on the bad days when I lose one, or on the long deployments away from my own children. The look of gratitude in that father's eyes, the blind trust of his children, and the ability to make a difference in someone's life. A simple gesture of kindness. An overwhelming gesture of gratitude. I did not choose a career in medicine. I was called to it . . . by two small children and their father in Kenya, many years ago.

—Jason Unruh, Navy Corpsman

Often military medical personnel are tasked with humanitarian missions worldwide, whether it's to care for foreign nationals who don't have access to adequate treatment, or Americans living and working abroad.

"That's Not Paul!"

In January of 2013, I was put on alert for a "secret mission" to Africa. Funny thing is CNN knew before me that there was a patient my team had to pick up in Algeria. As I was waiting for the plane to button up on the tarmac at Ramstein Air Base in Germany, I was reading the news on my iPhone. CNN stated that an American C-17 with an onboard medical team was on their way. Holy shit, that was my team! CNN reported that there had been a gas plant hostage situation and there were casualties.

From 2006 to 2013, I was on a medical unit known as a critical care air transport team (CCATT), composed of my doctor, a respiratory therapist, and myself, the registered nurse. We were told an American civilian worker in Algeria needed critical care assistance. Because he worked at a gas plant, we naturally assumed his injuries were either related to inhalation of gas fumes, or possibly burns. We did not know the mechanism of the injury, his age, or current status. We had to prepare for the worst, and loaded coolers of O-negative blood, fresh frozen plasma, and anything else a young trauma surgeon would need. We were literally a flying emergency room.

We arrived in Algiers, and after much confusion, the local government said our patient was deceased, from cardiac arrest. After learning what had actually transpired at the gas plant, we seriously doubted he died of a simple cardiac arrest. We all felt that horrific trauma from a gunshot was more likely. With no patient to care for, I was "off shift," just waiting to return to Germany, but while our security team waited for the body, we were cautioned not to leave the plane because it was too dangerous, though we weren't exactly sure why.

As I looked out from the tail of the C-17, the Algerian airport looked like a shopping stampede on Black Friday. There was a mob that desperately wanted to be on that plane; the majority of them were the gas plant workers who had escaped. But what were they escaping from? They ran to the only place they knew, the airport, though initially they were not allowed to approach our transport plane sitting on the runway, getting refueled, and still waiting for the body of the deceased American.

With clearance from the big cheese in Washington, DC, we were able to take a few of them back with us. Apparently, some countries wanted their citizens to stay put and wouldn't grant them permission to leave, at least not with us. One by one, those allowed to leave walked onto the plane; I immediately noticed the blank expressions of relief on each face.

They practically collapsed anywhere they could find to sit. I was mesmerized. I took the opportunity to speak with a few who spoke English, as the pine box with our American citizen was boarded and strapped to the floor in front of the men I was speaking with.

"That's not Paul!"

No, it wasn't Paul. I knew the name of the deceased; I reassured the group that it was not Paul. I then asked them, "Who was Paul?"

"We were told an American civilian worker in Algeria needed critical care assistance. Because he worked at a gas plant, we naturally assumed his injuries were either related to inhalation of gas fumes, or possibly burns. . . . We had to prepare for the worst, and loaded coolers of O-negative blood, fresh frozen plasma, and anything else a young trauma surgeon would need. We were literally a flying emergency room." AIR FORCE PHOTO

Paul was the American who was in a group of five men who planned an escape after a band of terrorists seized the gas plant where they worked. As I looked at their ripped jeans and superficial cuts from the barbed wire, they told me the amazing story of their escape.

Three days prior, the siege occurred when the group of five were in their dorm rooms. They were from the UK, New Zealand, Ireland, Japan, and the USA respectively; Paul was the now missing American. All of them were engineers of some sort. They were dirty, hungry, tired, and still in a state of shock, though I still didn't know why.

The engineer from the UK or Ireland, I can't remember which, was speaking a mile a minute. He needed a good swig of whiskey and a cigarette to calm him down, but neither of those were on board and I felt helpless not being able to "sedate" him. As an ICU nurse, sedating our patients was in our control and it "sedated" us, the CCAT team, because seeing the pain, confusion, and fear when a patient is aroused from their sedation with a breathing tube in their throat is difficult.

They all tried to speak to me at the same time, almost desperate to tell someone, so I heard fragments of something awful transpiring over the previous three days. When terrorists were overrunning the plant, word traveled quickly between the group via text messages. The five decided to hunker down in their dorms with locked doors, seeking refuge under their beds. One shared a story that a terrorist was walking the dorm hallway, saying that everyone but any Americans were free to leave and basically was shouting out, "Come out come out wherever you are."

Since he was not an American, the Brit contemplated coming out, but either he was warned not to via text or heard gunshots and screaming himself. It did not matter what country the workers were from; the terrorists were killing anybody who was not on their side. He stayed put, and the five of them used text messages to come up with a plan of escape.

They knew where there were weaknesses in the barbed wire that protected the perimeter of the gas plant. Eventually, after two days trapped under their bunks with no food, peeing in bottles, they all decided to meet up at a predetermined location. Everybody but Paul showed up. They couldn't wait. They all knew they had to leave and hoped Paul would show up at the airport, their final destination to get out of Algeria.

Terrorists from the Algerian Al Qaeda Brigade, led by Mokhtar Belmokhtar, seized a gas plant and took several foreigners as hostages, including one American. UNITED NATIONS WATCH GROUP PHOTO

The story gets crazier, and I couldn't imagine how lucky they were to be sitting on that plane with me. As the four approached the airport, a car bomb exploded. Initially they thought they were the targets. However, the bomb was a dud and a man emerged from the car and went inside the airport with the four gas plant engineers. Gunmen pursued the car bomb victim and he was finished off right in front of the engineers!

The gunmen then barricaded themselves in some office at the airport, and the Algerian police fired machine guns through the door and walls of this office rather than storm the room. I was shocked listening to this story, because I rarely ever had the opportunity to have patients share the gory details that led up to me meeting them.

Most of my patients were heavily sedated by the time they were loaded on board for transport back to Germany. It immediately made me appreciate that I hopefully would never find myself in a predicament where everything except oxygen is taken away from me, against my will. After being deployed four times, the first days before the war kicked off in March 2003, I realized I never had the opportunity to really share the moment with people who comprehended getting a second chance at life.

Since I had nothing to do during the flight back to Germany, there was prime real estate next to the patient that was not Paul. I sat next to "not Paul" and reflected on what I experienced in my life up to that point. For weeks afterward, I scoured the news looking for Paul myself, relieved that he never was mentioned as one of our dead. I hope Paul eventually caught up with his colleagues. To this day, after many missions to several war zones, caring for too many casualties to ever forget, I still think about Paul.

—Air Force Capt. Jackie Richards

HOME FRONT

When war starts, a soldier wants like hell to be there, but once he's there, he wants like hell to come home.

—Anonymous

The final months before shipping out to war are bittersweet, for those doing the leaving, and for those they leave behind. Every moment is precious, knowing it may be their last together. Training is at a fever pitch, getting units ready to work as a cohesive team when the bullets start flying . . . when the pucker factor kicks in. But preparing to go into battle is a serious business and often during training exercises—designed to simulate actual combat conditions—mistakes are made and the participants get hurt, sometimes seriously. As such, medical personnel are prepositioned nearby, ready to rush in and utilize the life-saving skills they'd been trained for.

At the same time, combatants are getting the shots they need to ward off all those nasty diseases in the Mideast, getting their financial and personal affairs in order, taking time off to spend time with loved ones, everyone unsure if they will get back home, alive, and with all appendages still attached. Many are getting prepped for deployment for the first time, but for many others it's just the latest in the string. There are others who have cast aside the accoutrements of war and traded them in for more important things they now need to survive.

Instead of body armor, Kevlar, and their weapons, they now rely on crutches or a wheelchair, prosthetics, and maybe a service dog to help them cope with a new battle . . . living the day to day life as a disabled veteran. For many of these former combatants, the scars of war are clearly evident—the amputations, paralysis, disfiguring burns, blindness, etc. But for others, the scars of war are invisible but just as debilitating: posttraumatic stress and traumatic brain injuries. And for their loved ones, it can get overwhelming, and sadly, some cut and run, never looking back, leaving the veteran to fend for themselves.

They may have returned home, but the war continues to follow them, haunt them. Tragically for some, the war follows them all the way to the grave.

❧

Training missions are intended to simulate combat conditions, and as such, sometimes casualties occur, which is why it's so important to have medical personnel onsite during live-fire exercises, physical fitness tests, and, in this case, a nighttime parachute jump.

Drop Zone Coverage

When I was younger I used to believe in luck, chance, and fate. Then, as I matured and gained more experience, I started seeing connections, links, and purposes in our lives. I believe we are all connected, whether good or bad, by events and circumstances that bring us together for the collective human experience.

July 2001 was an extremely hot and humid North Carolina summer, and for one week I was assigned as the medical officer charged with providing medical coverage of parachute drop zones. This is rotational duty that is commonly shared among airborne infantry battalion physician assistants; basically we cover airborne operations for each other's units. Only one health care provider is assigned per parachute drop. With my team of combat medics and the drop zone safety team, we would cover parachute drop zones for large-scale nighttime airborne operations. These airborne operations consisted of seven hundred or more military parachutists dropped in the span of about 60 seconds. Most of the injuries we take care of at the drop zone are sprains and strains, but the potential for an accident is ever-present. Nighttime airborne operations also add a different dimension to parachute operations due to fear, uncertainty, and decreased depth perception.

The first night of medical coverage was a dark, quiet, humid, and misty summer night. One of the methods we used to medically cover a large parachute drop zone was to split it into sections and man each sector with combat medics carrying trauma equipment and radios. We would typically set up the main element of the drop zone safety team at the north end of the drop zone, and this is where I would position myself with our military ambulances.

We familiarized ourselves with the drop zone itself, which was mostly open sand with slightly rolling hills and scattered vegetation consisting of

American paratroopers wait for the green light to jump. In July of 2001, more than seven hundred soldiers descended on a North Carolina training site. ARMY PHOTO

scrub oak. It was surrounded by one-hundred-foot pine trees on the east and west sides and bordered by two roads on the north and south sides.

The basic plan was that after the military parachutists had exited the aircraft, we would begin our sweep of the drop zone with roving foot medics and military ambulances, searching for any casualties.

As the C-130 transport planes began to approach the drop zone, we heard the low rumble, almost like distant thunder, and we stood by in anticipation and hoped there would be no injuries. We could barely see the multiple aircraft approaching because of the low clouds and misty weather conditions. The first aircraft pass would release a large amount of equipment, mostly vehicles and artillery pieces. The next pass of multiple aircraft would drop the parachutists, around seven hundred personnel.

After the personnel drop, our medical team began to sweep the drop zone by foot and vehicle for any casualties. At the same time, the misty conditions turned into a dense fog. I sat at the north end of the drop zone with one combat medic in a military ambulance listening to the radio for any updates of injured personnel and awaiting any casualties. After about ten minutes of radio silence, for some reason I began to get worried. I felt something was odd or amiss. I then decided to have my medic drive us around the drop zone in order to get some ground truth.

We started moving south in the drop zone. About five minutes into our drive, I saw through the mist a parachute unfurling like a flag on the ground. This was a strange sight, because each parachutist is instructed to pack their used parachutes into bags and carry them to a collection area.

As I approached the area, I noted a soldier at the end parachute barely responsive and moaning. We released his harness and my medic began to get intravenous access as I continued my quick survey of the patient. From my quick scan I believed he might have a pelvic fracture, a potentially devastating injury. A person can lose their whole blood volume in the space that is created by the fracture and expire. We then tightened a sheet around the patient's pelvis and placed him on a backboard because I was concerned about a possible spinal injury.

Normally it requires four personnel to carry a patient, so it was especially difficult for just the two of us. To load the patient I basically had to clean and jerk one side of the patient and litter, hold it in the air while the medic got underneath and stabilized that end of the litter, then I went to the other end and again clean and jerked it so we could walk the patient over to the ambulance and load him up. Throughout this movement, we continued to comfort and reassure him.

It was no easy task for the two of us to load a full-grown man onto a military ambulance on a military stretcher, but we could not wait for others because we knew he was in extremis and we were working against the clock to save him.

After we had him secured in the ambulance, we moved back to the north end of the drop zone to the rest of the safety team. All the while, the weather conditions were getting worse with more mist and fog rolling in, and I knew an evacuation by air ambulance would not be possible. As I approached the drop zone safety team, I told the noncommissioned officer in charge that we had a patient who was dying and I was going to take him directly to the hospital, and then instructed him to close the drop zone to prevent any further parachute operations.

I could have sent a medic with him to the ER, but I knew this patient might not survive the trip, and if something happened, such as traumatic arrest or worse, I did not want one of my medics to have carried the burden or responsibility of a patient dying under their care or watch.

The drive to the hospital was about thirty minutes, and during that time we continued to talk and comfort the patient. We brought him straight into the emergency department, turned him over to the staff, then went back to the drop zone to assist with any further casualties. As a safety precaution, when the full complement of medical personnel and safety team is not present, the drop zone cannot remain "open," so it was important to get back onsite.

The next day I learned the patient had a parachute malfunction, slammed into the ground, and sustained a significant pelvic fracture. He had required many units of blood. I went to visit him in the intensive care unit at our hospital, where he was sedated and on a ventilator. It was there I received the update of the patient's condition. I also met his wife. When we met she said I looked familiar to her, and I brushed off her

Seven hundred paratroopers in sixty seconds, at night. The darkness adds "a different dimension to parachute operations due to fear, uncertainty, and decreased depth perception." DOD PHOTO

comment saying I get that remark all the time. Later that day the patient was transferred to a higher level of care because of continued bleeding due to his significant pelvic fracture. That was the last I heard of the patient until about two weeks later.

I received a call from my boss stating the patient had been transferred back to our hospital after receiving treatment at a large trauma center, and he and his family wanted me to visit them. As I walked in the room later that morning to see them, the paratrooper was there with his wife and his son.

"From my quick scan I believed he might have a pelvic fracture, a potentially devastating injury. A person can lose their whole blood volume in the space that is created by the fracture and expire. . . . The drive to the hopsital was about thirty minutes." ARMY PHOTO

He thanked me for saving his life and then told me his story of that fateful night. He said he had a parachute malfunction and had hit the ground very hard. He knew he was dying. In what he believed were his last moments he told me, "I called out in Jesus's name . . . save me." He then told me an angel appeared out of the darkness and it was me. I assured him I was no angel, just doing my job, and I appreciated his thanks.

His wife then said she knew exactly who I was. Earlier the same day of her husband's accident, I had seen her son in the clinic as a patient. At the time it was just a routine doctor's visit, but looking back, she felt it was fate. She then started to cry and said she did not believe this was by accident. God had intervened to ensure I took care of her husband that night. She truly believed that, and since then, I look back at this incident as pivotal in shaping and changing my beliefs as well. After this incident I began to believe that wherever I am, I am there for a purpose.

—George A. Barbee

Some veterans puff up their war stories, claiming to be someone they're not. Many more never say a word about what they've been through, what they've endured, because it's too horrific to remember. Some carry invisible scars, such as posttraumatic stress and traumatic brain injury. For others—hobbling around on crutches, tooling around in a wheelchair—it's clearly evident they've been through hell. Jackie Mansueto encountered one such soldier during her duty as a pharmacy tech. He turned out to be more than just another of the many who came to her for their medications.

Everyone Is a Hero

One particularly exhausting day, I was sent to the front desk window at the hospital to check patients in. I wasn't feeling it that day and would have preferred to just be filling prescriptions back in the pharmacy where I would be out of sight, all by myself. But instead, patient after patient bombarded my window, each with their own special problem or strange request. I was tackling everything the best I could. The next person to check in was a soldier in civilian attire. He was very direct, which was refreshing to me. No chitchat or beating around the bush. Then I noticed his prescription was to treat severe pain. Some very heavy meds. I saw him wincing a bit so I asked him if he was okay and he very calmly and nonchalantly replied, "Yeah, I got my leg blown off while I was deployed a couple of months ago."

I've been working in military medicine for over a decade now and I've seen numerous amputees, including quadriplegics. However, this particular soldier startled me with his casual response. It was like he was saying, "Yeah, I know I was seriously injured and I can either complain about it or keep pressing on and make the best of it." The fact that he was also in civilian clothing really forced me to do some soul searching, and rethink how I interact with others. He looked like your average guy: blue jeans and a T-shirt, mid-twenties, and clean cut. But he was anything but average. He was what I call an "everyday hero." I know when he divulged that info to me, he wasn't boasting about his war injury, just simply stating what happened, and doing his best to deal with the consequences.

This one inconspicuous, ordinary-looking guy changed the way I dealt with patients from then on. I now realize every single patient has a story. They might not openly reveal it to anyone else, but it's there. The widow who's grumpy and scowls at everyone and doesn't talk much.

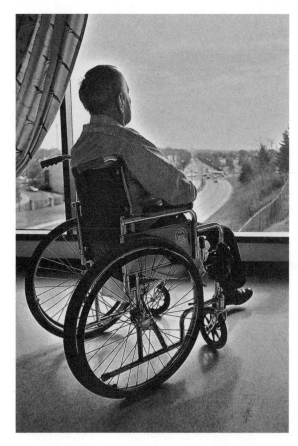

Many veterans handle their injuries with quiet dignity, a nonchalance that masks the hardships they've endured.
PHOTO BY GARY BLOOMFIELD

The old-timer stooped over and wearing his World War II ball cap, who used to be a fighter pilot and probably lost more buddies than he can count. The infant who will never meet their father killed in action. The active duty member who is recovering from the injuries and trauma of his most recent fourteen-month deployment.

If I do have the opportunity to check in patients now, I treat it as an honor. It is my pleasure to serve every patient who has sacrificed so much for our country, and in their own way they all have made sacrifices. It doesn't matter if they are active duty in uniform or a family of dependents. Every single one of them deserves the best of me. Always.

—Jackie Mansueto

For our nation's wounded warriors recovering from debilitating injuries sustained on distant battlefields, sometimes small victories, such as a simple smile, or a first step, are worth celebrating.

The Silly String Ambush

It was the twinkle in his eye that caught my attention, and the start of a curve upward of his mouth that turned into a full smile that stopped me in place. It had been two months since the lance corporal had been medevac'd in, and this was the first sign of his personality coming through. I had entered the doorway and had tripped over my shoe, the floor, who knows, but I had stumbled forward, caught myself all the while juggling several items I was carrying in, to keep them from hitting the floor. This was most amusing to this Marine, but more amazing to me and to his dad who was also in the room was that this was the first time he had smiled post-injury.

Little did we know that this would be the start of a host of practical jokes and opportunities to insert his brand of humor into the world he found himself. We will call him Marine Fred (not because I do not wish to use his real name but for the sake of his personal privacy and his right to own his own story). There is a good-humored rivalry that occurs between people who have served in differing branches of our military, and it is no different for the wounded. I am not sure who got the bigger kick out of this good-natured banter—the servicemen or their families. As Fred began to progress and heal from his injuries, he became more and more interested in stirring up some shenanigans on the ward. This Marine would enlist the assistance of staff, or his family, and organize a group of other wounded servicemen to carry out "stealth raids" into Army territory or Navy territory. These missions would take days to plan and prepare. His first target was the 1st Cavalry soldier next to his room. He planted a USMC flag front and center of the soldier's bed. Another mission was to plant a CD player rigged to play the USMC song when the soldier entered his own room. Of course this initiated a counteroffensive that involved an "Army Parking Only" sign placed above Fred's bed and a US Army blanket placed over his sheets.

This went on over the months and was a great morale booster, but the mother of all operations came to be called the Silly String Ambush. The planning for this became very elaborate and involved recreational therapy, physical therapy, speech therapy, nursing staff, and every service member who could participate being involved. Rec therapy assisted Fred in planning an outing to a store where he could purchase the silly string canisters. Physical therapy assisted him in how to hold the can to get maximum distance, speech therapy assisted on the timing of the ambush, and the nurses? Well, we just hoped to not get caught in the crossfire.

The day of the mission Fred was so excited he could hardly contain his smile. He had been looking forward to "go time" for about three weeks. The timing was crucial and everything in both the Marine's day and the soldier's day had to line up just right for this to work. This was going to be big . . . like the Army-Navy game, bragging rights were at stake! Little did Fred know that his plan had been leaked, the soldier had pretty good intelligence about the ambush, and he had been doing some prep of his own and had a small arsenal of water pistols at the ready.

The clock struck at the top of the hour, the ward doors banged open, and in rolled 1st Cav, in his wheelchair, water pistols at the low ready. From around the corner wheeled in the Corps with his can of silly string at the high ready. His band of raiders commenced firing silly string and 1st Cav was covered from head to toe, a mass of pink, blue, neon green, and yellow goo! He blasted Fred with a few rounds of water, and his family assisted in extricating him from the immediate threat. 1st regrouped and just when the Corps thought they had the battle won he counterattacked with dogged resolve and managed to completely soak Fred from head to toe. The whole ward was a mess! The laughter and energy created by this mission lasted for days. The memory of that day will last a lifetime.

The official proclamation was that the contest ended in a draw, and the two combatants met in the middle of the ward, shook hands, and agreed to up the ante for the next time they met in battle. Their silly string and water pistols were never far from their sides. Those moments were opportunities to see these tough, battle-scarred, and war-hardened nineteen- and twenty-year-olds let loose, create their version of normal, and to occupy their thoughts and time with fun. For me this was like a gift to be placed in my memory, to be tugged out and remembered when times got tough and the weight of our mission became heavy. A slight smile tugs at my own lips as I put my words to paper and remember a Marine named Fred who dreamed of a mission filled with silly string.

—Connie Bengston, BSN, RN, PHN

Leaving the war behind is not as simple as turning in weapons and equipment, and discarding boots and uniforms too ragged and filthy to ever get clean. The emotional toll, the nightmares, and flashbacks can often haunt a combat veteran for years. And sometimes a smell—gunpowder or grilled meat—the sound of a car backfiring or fireworks, or the sight of someone who reminds them of their former adversary can remind them of the mission they left behind to neutralize all enemies, foreign and domestic.

Murderous Thoughts

One day in 2004 I remember we got a number of casualties from Iraq who were sent to Bethesda, where they were evaluated and sent directly to the Naval Hospital at Camp Lejeune. At the time Bethesda was pretty full and these were stable patients—mostly orthopedic who needed ongoing care and rehabilitation. Many of them arrived to us only three to four days after their initial injury in Iraq. One of the young Marines was taken back to the operating room and was put under general anesthesia for a wash out and debridement of both leg and arm wounds.

After his surgery he was brought to our post-anesthesia recovery unit. I was in the PACU evaluating another patient and noticed this patient in the next bed becoming more alert and staring at his orthopedic surgeon, who had his back to the patient and was leaning over a bedside table writing post-op orders. His orthopedic surgeon had dark hair and a complexion that looked Middle Eastern.

The patient's eyes were fixated on the orthopedic surgeon's, and I watched the patient sit up and quietly and methodically start scooting to the end of his bed, moving his bandaged arm and his leg that was wrapped in a large splint without making a sound. The patient's jaw was set, his nose was flaring a little, and there was an intensity in his face that made me think he was getting ready to attack the surgeon who had just operated on him. I called for help, and the surgeon turned; the patient was clearly disoriented and became agitated, so we sedated him with medications. When he woke almost an hour later, he remembered none of the events. We see this behavior in some of our patients—it's as though they are not in the room with us but are thousands of miles away.

—Necia Williams

To be young and in love, while planning a lifetime together, with the world and all its trimmings just waiting to be enjoyed, is a couple's dream. But often a deployment overseas postpones those plans.

She too was marking off the days. Just eighteen days, then they could kickstart the dreams they'd put on hold when he got deployed to Iraq. They could have gone ahead with the wedding before he left, but didn't want to rush it. But then that night his parents called—actually it was his dad who explained what happened, but she could hear his mom crying in the background. It was bad news. The worst. All he could say was that his son—her knight in shining armor—was still alive. And he'd be coming home a few days earlier, just not the way they'd hoped. Instead of the airport, they'd see him when he got to the ICU. They'd call once they knew more but warned her that he'd need years of surgery and rehab.

At some point during the call, she felt light-headed. His dad didn't know much more but would keep her informed, let her know when they could go see him. The next morning she thought maybe she'd had a bad dream. But then she saw the notepad next to the phone. She'd scribbled only a few words: "He's alive. Extensive surgeries. Prosthetics. Wheelchair. Home early."

It wasn't a bad dream. It was the rest of their lives together. She waited till after breakfast and called her maid of honor to tell her the news . . . and let her know the wedding was off.

She Walked Away When He Needed Her the Most

Early morning phone calls that disrupt our sleep are never a good thing. This particular morning, my husband and I were woken up by a call from our Marine Corps brother. He informed us that one of our close Marine brothers had committed suicide just as he had reached his new duty station. My husband and I were in the middle of moving to a new house and were groggy as we struggled to wake up.

As we gathered our thoughts and hung up the phone, my husband took a deep sigh and asked, "Is this a bad dream?" We got up and started packing again in disbelief. As the day went on, we needed to go on base to pick up our moving trailer from the recreation check out there. I agreed.

As we were driving to the base, we stopped at the light just outside the front gate. To the right of the intersection we noticed two eighteen-wheelers. One was carrying two Humvees with heavy armored plating and bullet-resistant glass. The second was carrying a Husky, as the Marines call it, which is used to detect improvised explosive devices, or IEDs, which are embedded in the ground and detonated, typically when an American convoy passes close by.

My eyes fixated on the transports and I was lost in thought, staring as they passed in front of our car, slowly making their way onto the base. I somehow was able to put my deep emotions into words and said to my husband, "Every time I see those things I get so sad inside."

I was instantly thrown back to a time when I took care of the wounded warriors who came to Brooke Army Medical Center in San Antonio. I remember standing in the receiving bay as a member of the team of nurses waiting for the flight. These wounded warriors would be flown in from their point of contact to our receiving bay within two to three days.

There are no words to describe the feeling standing in that receiving bay waiting for these heroes to roll in. Everyone is silent, and sometimes there is a faint sound of the doctors typing their last-minute orders into the computer. When the wounded warriors come in it is a complete adrenaline rush, loud and chaotic. I started to think about one wounded warrior in particular who was just nineteen years old. He had been involved in an IED blast, and I had been assigned to him. It wasn't my first assignment like this, but what made it so striking to me was that he was the youngest.

I can still remember sitting in the briefing early that morning. We had been notified from the last shift that his parents and his girlfriend had flown in and were waiting for him to arrive on our ward. As a nurse

A heavy equipment transporter: "Every time I see those things I get so sad. . . ." These behemoths are bound to a war zone . . . convoy duty, which means ambushes and improvised explosive devices, machine-gun bullets stitching windows and armor plating. Casualties. DOD PHOTO

and patient advocate, you become emotionally attached to your patients. When sitting in the report room, the nurse giving the updates paints a verbal picture of the patient you are assigned to and at that moment you start to become emotionally invested.

This is a person, not just a patient, who you are going to help bring back to life, and you will do whatever it takes to accomplish that daunting mission. You are their advocate and will carry out the doctors' orders, but will also facilitate additional orders to get them the help they need to accomplish whole mind, body, and spiritual healing.

My initial reaction was to shield him, and I personally felt his nineteen-year-old girlfriend should not have come. Not so soon. I had been briefed that my patient was a triple amputee, was having pain control issues, and was still very groggy from heavy pain medications. When the pain was unbearable, doctors would have to give him light sedatives. This had happened several times within the three days since the time of impact, and the doctors and nurses had been struggling to stabilize him throughout his journey from overseas to our facility in San Antonio.

As we walked out of the report room, our first task was to get the pain under control as we received the patients from the inbound flight. I really felt the girlfriend should not see him just yet. You realize how young they are, just teenagers. They had their whole future in front of them, but now their plans were dramatically changed. Even though the health care team will do whatever is necessary to get back the life he had before, he will never be the same. Their life will never be what they hoped. As you learn how to take care of these patients, you start to realize how the family is never prepared to walk into that room for the first time. Never.

Sometimes it takes these wounded warriors several days, sometimes weeks to even realize where they are as they come out of the fog of heavy pain medications and sedatives. If you have ever been really injured and hurting in the hospital, family can be a great support system. Sometimes it is not the best decision to have friends come and see you at your worst. Sometimes medical staff get a bad feeling if we find out the girlfriend wants to see the patient, and we remain reserved and cautious. Too often they will be there for a little while, but soon will drift away. Some are never seen again.

Other couples met and hugged at the airport. She had to see him at the hospital and couldn't handle it. "They had their whole future in front of them, but now their plans were dramatically changed. Even though the health care team will do whatever is necessary to get back the life he had before, he will never be the same."AIR FORCE PHOTO

This is an added burden, another wound the patient is left to deal with during their most trying times. There are so many facets to healing, and sometimes, all they need is their close family.

As we brought him up to the ward, we stabilized him for a few minutes before allowing his family and girlfriend into the room. They were all very emotional—stunned, shocked, horrified, heartbroken. His mother instantly rushed toward him and held his shoulder and hand and sobbed. His father on the other side of the bed laid his hand on his head. His girlfriend stood at the foot of the bed and gave a smile and waved. He was happy to see her but put his head back. We left them to bond. Within fifteen minutes the parents and girlfriend came out of the room and said their son was in extreme pain. The team rushed in and began to administer his sedative medications. The young man fell back asleep from the heavy medications. While we busied ourselves with the request, I noticed the parents were talking to his girlfriend, who was very upset, emotionally distraught. She was very sorry for what had happened, but she could not continue with the relationship. It was all too overwhelming for her. She would be on the next flight home.

This conversation took place in front of the nurses' station. His parents were very understanding and consoling toward her. They assured her that she would go on good terms and thanked her for coming out to see him. For me, it all unfolded in slow motion as the young girl looked to the floor with tears falling from her face and she turned away to leave. The parents watched her leave the ward and then turned to go back into their son's room. What would they say to him? How would it affect him? So many emotions go through your mind, watching someone else's life drastically change before your eyes. You can feel their pain, sorrow, frustrations, anger, and sympathy. As the days unfolded, I experienced and helped them get through the rollercoaster of grief followed with small doses of happiness when their son made progress, and then back into the pain, sorrow, and frustrations as the healing process tumbled from one day to the next.

As time passed, the young man began to settle into a pain medication regimen that seemed to control the pain enough for him to start eating. On his fifth day on the ward, it was lunchtime and I was walking into his room with his lunch tray. He seemed to be more alert and more comfortable than before.

His parents were asleep in chairs next to his bed. He lifted his head slightly as I walked into the room. I smiled and said, "Your lunch is here, I'll help you sit up so you can eat." He said okay. We started to position him and he was still having a lot of pain, even though it was bearable now. The physical therapist had been working with him, and he was learning how to use his one arm to reposition himself.

As we were working together to get him in position to try to eat, he asked if we could stop for a minute. I said sure, and he just put his head back in frustration. I said, "Is there anything I can do to help you? Do you need more pain medications?" He looked over at me and asked, "Will I have to take pain medications for the rest of my life?" I smiled and said,

"I'm sure that would not be the case and the doctors feel you will make a good recovery." He did not return my smile and asked, "Am I going to need someone to take care of me all the time like this?" I reminded him of the therapist who told him what a good job he was doing and he would progress fast. I smiled to cheer him up, but still, no positive response. Then, looking dead into my eyes he asked me bluntly: "Why am I like this? Why am I still alive?"

I was startled and couldn't look away, knowing he was waiting for an answer. I even looked over to his parents for help, but they were asleep, exhausted after so many days remaining at his side. I felt the pain in his eyes, and I saw the deepness of his soul as he stared at me, waiting for an answer. Waiting for me to say something. I hoped he was only venting his frustrations, and would eventually look away, but as the uncomfortableness of his glare held me, stunned, he waited. As I searched for an answer, he did not break eye contact. What am I going to say? I could not honestly say everything will be okay. His life will be determined by his injuries. My heart was broken. I grabbed his hand.

When a person goes through the transformation of becoming a Marine, you learn to trust the Marine next to you more than you have trusted anyone else in your entire life. The bonds formed are never broken. You understand each other more deeply than anyone else, you feel each other's happiness more deeply than anyone else, and your soul hurts as if it was you experiencing their pain. You become closer than brothers and sisters. I have never felt this bond in any aspect of the civilian world, except when I'm working with these wounded warriors.

At that moment, I felt his overwhelming pain, the kind no one can explain unless you have experienced what they go through. It is one thing to be sympathetic; it is another to understand their pain from personal experience. I was forever changed at that moment. I was infused with a new appreciation for life. How delicate and precious life is. How it can be instantly changed. I learned about hopelessness. I learned about hope. I searched for the meaning of life and tried to understand better what our goal here on earth might be.

I prayed to Jesus for answers and learned about God's answers to our life's questions. I learned how to provide hope for those who feel there is

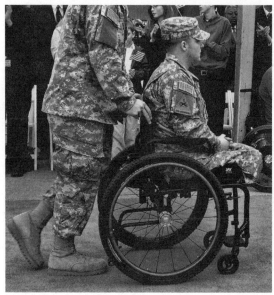

". . . looking dead into my eyes he asked me bluntly: 'Why am I like this? Why am I still alive?' I was startled and couldn't look away, knowing he was waiting for an answer. I even looked over to his parents for help, but they were asleep, exhausted after so many days remaining at his side. I felt the pain in his eyes, and I saw the deepness of his soul as he stared at me, waiting for an answer. Waiting for me to say something." DOD PHOTO

no hope. I learned how to encourage them to continue on and let them know there is always hope. These wounded warriors carry honor like no one will ever comprehend. Yet for them to carry that honor is a heavy burden. Some get lost in the shadow of their honor and can no longer see the light. Sometimes they may feel their sacrifices are not appreciated. If they do not have that simple support of loved ones, then what have they sacrificed so much for?

I feel it is everyone's duty to help that person in your life who struggles in this way, to grab their hand and pull them to the light again. It is also everyone's duty to ensure they are given gratitude for their intense sacrifices for our country.

My patient was in the hospital for four months and sixteen days. When he was discharged, we had a little celebration for him. He had thanked all of us for helping him find hope. He told us: "Because of you all, I am able to go home. I have hope and I know I'll be able to continue on." To hear him say that has seared my soul forever. That is now my goal in this life. I will never allow someone to lose sight of the light of hope. Not on my watch.

The light turned green and my husband began driving through the intersection. My mind came back to the reality of being in the car and not with my patient those many years ago. As we drove behind those eighteen-wheelers, tears started falling from my eyes. I felt sorrow for those who might someday be in this Humvee that would carry him into harm's way. Talking to my husband, I said, "You just want to reach out and embrace them all, to keep them safe and never let them go."

In dealing with the loss of our Marine Corps brother, we who served together have recently formed a contact circle and are sending pictures of the memories we had together with him. We have all vowed to reach out to each other if we feel down and to never allow this to happen again.

—Shanell Almaguer

For combat veterans who've been downrange for months, they think of very few things when they're not busy trying to stay alive. They smoke and joke about what they plan to do when they get back to "the world."

Positive Attitude

It was late Monday morning when the young Marine finally regained consciousness. He found himself in agonizing pain in the base hospital's ICU, with tubes up every fundamental orifice, wires monitoring every function, and a gorgeous nurse hovering over him. He remembered he'd been in a hell of a firefight a few days prior, but had no idea how he got to where he was at that moment, or how bad his injuries were.

The nurse gave the combat Marine a serious, deep look straight into the eyes, and he heard her slowly say, "You may not feel anything from the waist down."

The little twitch in his pants reminded him that he'd been in combat a really long time and it had been far too long since he'd seen a female. Somehow, despite the heavy painkillers that made him woozy, he managed to mumble in reply, "Well then, can I feel your tits?"

And that, God bless him, is what is called a positive attitude!

—Dr. Twisted

The birth of a child should be the most joyous moment in a young couple's life. But when one of them is serving overseas in a combat zone, there is very real fear that something might happen to snatch that joy away.

Tears in the Delivery Room

After returning from my last trip to Iraq, I was on duty in the hospital one night when I got called to provide anesthesia for a caesarean section. There was a young woman whose baby was not tolerating labor well. She was very stoic and did not display the usual range of emotions. Her mother was at her side and would be coming to the operating room with her. This was not a particularly unusual occurrence at Camp Lejeune, because Marine fathers are sometimes deployed when their children are born.

I explained to my patient and her mother what would be occurring from an anesthesia standpoint in the operating room. The safest anesthetic for this patient was for her to have a spinal and be awake for the birth of her son. She had no questions and continued to have an expressionless face and tone of voice.

When I left to talk with her obstetrician and the labor nurse, I learned that her husband had been killed in Iraq the month before. I informed the OR crew of the patient's situation and the fact that her husband had recently been killed to prevent the crew from saying anything like "Let's get pictures so you can send them to Dad." The patient was very cooperative but still stoic while being moved to the OR, having monitors attached to her, and placing the spinal. Once the obstetrician had scrubbed and gowned and we checked to make sure that the spinal had set up, the surgery began.

The patient's mother sat in a chair near the patient's head and stroked her daughter's forehead and talked quietly and gently to her, with the sound of the monitor in the background going "beep beep beep" with each beat of the patient's heart. Within a few minutes the surgeon called out "skin" to indicate that the surgery had begun (skin had been cut),

It should have been the happiest moment for the young mother, but all she could do was cry, because her husband, a Marine, had been killed in Iraq a month earlier. TAMPA GENERAL HOSPITAL

then over the next several minutes various instruments were called for followed by the word uterine indicating that uterine incision had been made.

A minute later a male infant was delivered and we all heard the cry of healthy newborn infant lungs. This was followed by the sound of the patient crying, which started quietly and continued to become heart-wrenching, grief-stricken sobs that became louder and louder with her body shaking.

Her mother rose out of her seat and reached down to hug and hold her daughter as best she could, given the fact that the surgical drapes extended up to the patient's underarm area. She held her like that, cradling her own baby, for the longest time while her daughter cried and cried.

I had tears in my own eyes, and when I looked over the drape I didn't see a dry eye in the room. After about ten minutes or so her baby was brought over so our patient could see her son before he went to the nursery. She seemed to calm a little, though she continued to cry for the longest time. I offered my patient medication to help her relax, but after talking with her mother she declined, and her mother told me that her daughter said she needed to cry.

I felt incredibly grateful that my patient's mother was there for her. I have a vast array of medications I can use to sedate patients, take away physical pain, make them not care about emotional pain, etc.; but in my entire arsenal, I had nothing that equaled a mother's love and support.

—Necia Williams

FINAL THOUGHTS

While working on several projects about America's war on terrorism and our wars in Iraq and Afghanistan, I decided I wanted to pay tribute to the medical personnel who care for our nation's wounded warriors. From the Navy corpsmen and combat medics accompanying our front-line troops and convoys, to everyone at aid stations and the field hospitals, on the dust-off flights and the Nightingale transports from the war zones, and the stateside military hospitals, burn wards, rehab centers, and VA hospitals, I sought to tell their story. Actually I wanted them to tell their own story . . . if I could just get them to sit still long enough to do it!

I quickly learned that many of these Type A personalities don't know how to slow down long enough to write about patients they can't forget. Even those who were willing to write something weren't sure if they could select just one patient from the hundreds, possibly thousands, they have cared for over many years.

For some who wrote stories for *The One*, they welcomed the task of recalling their patient and the events that unfolded while caring for them.

Robert G. Holcomb, who wrote "Mission to Kosovo and Back," wrote: "At the completion of the transport flight, we all felt like any marathon runner who experiences the post-race 'high,' a compilation of jubilation, relief, and a sense of tremendous pride. For me, reliving that flight today brings back that feeling, like a glorious reward for a job well done. In reality, it defines a passion all who do medical transport flights have, and validates we are truly following God's chosen path for us."

Col. Stanley Chartoff, who wrote "Richard"—and generously provided me with invaluable guidance in completing *The One*—explained the special bond those who work in military trauma medicine share and have a hard time leaving: "My testimonial to the importance of military medicine relates to a talk I heard at a military medical conference. I listened to a young female captain physician who concluded her talk with the story of an Air Force former pararescuer (PJ) missing a leg, who walked into her office, asking her to medically clear him to return to duty in pararescue—one of the Air Force's most difficult occupations recovering downed aircrew in hostile areas and providing emergency medical treatment.

"She could have told him it was hopeless, but instead she wrote his waiver and pushed it through. That airman was returned to the PJs and is now saving the lives of others. Knowing that young professionals like this Air Force captain are there to continue the tradition of military medicine makes me proud.

I reached out to hundreds in military trauma medicine, in collecting stories for *The One*. They all expressed interest in the project, though many said they either didn't feel comfortable with their writing skills, or couldn't find the time. Here's an example of just one message I received from a trauma surgeon who has served in both Iraq and Afghanistan: "I have a hundred stories, but I will send you the one that not only sticks in my mind and heart, but the one I can barely speak of without crying. I pray I am able to honor my hero appropriately with mere words." (Unfortunately, despite several promises to send in her story, this surgeon still didn't feel comfortable writing about the soldier who ended up being flown to Landstuhl Hospital in Germany, then stateside for follow-up surgeries and rehabilitation.)

Several doctors and nurses wanted to write about their tours in Iraq and Afghanistan, but that would divert from the theme of the book, which is remembering "The One" patient they can't forget: "I must confess it has taken a whole bunch of patient experiences to add up . . . not just one earth-shattering experience. As a group, the wounded warriors I took care of in Afghanistan remain the greatest inspiration."

With so many critically injured patients, an endless unbroken chain of carnage, was it easier to deal with if these care providers shut off their emotions?

Connie Bengston ("Learning to Run" and "The Silly String Ambush") wrote: "I entered each new assignment knowing it would cost, and it would take a toll, but still I did so every time with eagerness, wanting to be of service to those willing to sacrifice everything for our country. These are things we do not talk about as nurses. Our duty is to be care providers, and we are responsible to plan that care, to ensure each patient receives proper care, but it is never appropriate for us to truly 'care.' We all know that doing so is going to hurt emotionally. I knew that caring too much was going to break my heart, it was going to leave scars that may never be seen by others, but that was a price I was willing to pay for those who freely went in harm's way for me and for our country. I plan to continue to write and maybe at some point have something worthy to offer in the form of my own book. It might be painful sometimes, but whatever the outcome, it will be a journey that is necessary to complete."

One longtime trauma surgeon dispelled the impression that military doctors and nurses are just performing meatball surgery, and don't have any compassion for their patients, that they simply don't have time to care. "To me *all* of these brave troops have stood out in my mind as being something very special, especially those we could not successfully treat. It's very sad to see the youngest ones, who had a hopefully long life ahead, who had not really experienced living and never got the chance.

"Every night you just weep bitter tears, and pray for those they leave behind . . . parents, siblings, wives, girlfriends, children who will never know their dad or mom." (It was too emotionally draining for him to write a story for this book and I certainly understand.)

Every combatant who makes it to the aid station or field hospital is someone's son or daughter. They may be married, and they might have kids. Tragically many of them are mortally wounded, and so then it becomes a priority to keep them on life support and get them home as quickly as possible, so their families can see them one last time:

"Writing about my one patient stirred up a lot of memories," wrote **Trish Hayden**, author of "A Knife in the Head" and "The Best Job in the World." "I thought about the heroes we brought home to receive a higher echelon of care, and also of the ones we kept alive just long enough for the flight, so the families could say goodbye. After every deployment I come home thinking 'don't sweat the little things' because transporting wounded warriors is a reality check. After a while, things get back to normal and I start to let the little things bother me again. Writing this was a nice reality check . . . it reminded me that life is too short and we never know when it will be over." And a nurse who served in Iraq, wrote: "While deployed, I saw too many soldiers come through our ER. One evening I helped inventory the personal effects of a soldier. He had just returned to the war zone after a short trip home for some well-deserved leave. This particular situation triggered something and I went back to my room after my shift and wrote a letter to him apologizing for not being able to save him. I never wrote down his name due to patient confidentiality, but I think my apology was really for *all* the soldiers I could not save."

I found it interesting that this nurse took it personally that *she* couldn't save this and many other soldiers, even though an entire team of medical personnel are involved with the treatment of every patient. Still, she carries a heavy heart because *she* couldn't do more. As such, when one becomes one too many, compassion fatigue or burnout can take its toll.

Debra Berthold ("A Quiet Conversation") had a similar experience, and wrote about the young soldier who was killed in the Berlin disco bombing many years ago. Her job was to prep his body for transport to the States and list his possessions: "I don't think I truly understood what it meant to be a soldier until I had to deal with such a useless act of terrorism which took the life of a vibrant young man . . . who was the age my youngest son is now.

"Being able to write about the disco bombing and this soldier made me appreciate the fact that I have my sons, and there's a mother who hasn't had the joy of seeing hers become a husband and a father. I wish I could hug her. Even today, many years later, it still hurts to think about it. God bless our soldiers!"

All of the doctors, nurses, medics, and corpsmen who care for our wounded warriors have spouses and children of their own, so it's hard not to think about the family members back home, those whose lives are shattered by the loss of their military hero.

"Nobody wants to go to war, least of all the American serviceman," Dr. Holcomb wrote. "Sure, when commanded to or in the name of preserving our beloved country, we go in a heartbeat. Still, war is not a video game, war does not just involve soldiers, and death is the only certainty with war. For me, I get to see just how war affects the non-combatants, as they are referred to. I'm talking about the innocent children and their families. These are my patients during war. Taking care of kids affected by war carries a much deeper emotional scar. When my team is called in, it's as if we see our own children in each and every patient we transfer. The boy we moved out of Albania wasn't but a few years older than my son at the time. He began his day, a week earlier, heading out of the house to play. Unfortunately, the war-torn country of Albania was his playland.

"The memory of 'The One' for me will last a lifetime. I just wish I could engrain it into every world leader before they give the order, the declaration of war. War may be necessary, but make sure you know the total cost of war before giving any marching orders. Thank you for bringing our message to the rest of the world, and I look forward to continuing work with you in the future."

Remembering, at least for military medical personnel, isn't always a pleasant experience. Many have haunting memories, especially of the ones they couldn't save.

Lt. Col. Gail Fancher ("Three Special Guys, from the Many at Landstuhl") wrote: "The staff at Landstuhl sees the wounded at their worst. Many who arrive suffer from multiple injuries—"poly-trauma" so extensive that several teams of surgeons with different specialties— neurological, thoracic, ear and eye, facial reconstruction, and orthopedic, among others—may work on an individual patient, often simultaneously. Bodies are blown apart or crushed by IEDs, grenades, and suicide bombs, but so skillful are the medical teams there, so advanced the techniques and technology, Landstuhl's survival rate runs as high as 99.5 percent. (The survival rate among American wounded in World War II was 70 percent.) But all that success takes a toll. One of the little discussed but potent side effects of war is what's called combat and occupational stress reaction or secondary traumatic stress disorder. Compassion fatigue.

"After all the years of fighting in Iraq and Afghanistan, many of the doctors, nurses, and other staff at Landstuhl are exhausted or worse. Given what they've seen—the horrific wounds and amputations, the infections, agony, and grief—some walk around 'like zombies,'" one therapist said. Feelings of empathy and kindness yield to loneliness, despair, and burnout. Many of the compassion fatigue symptoms are similar to posttraumatic stress disorder (PTSD)—physical effects like headaches, gastrointestinal problems, reproductive troubles as well as mental—nightmares, flash-backs, anxiety, emotional distance, isolation, and more.

"Working with physically damaged men and women who are so deeply traumatized rubs off. The emotional rawness is contagious. A hospital handout on PTSD understatedly reads, 'When life-changing events occur, perceptions about the world may change. For example, before soldiers experience combat trauma, they may think the world is safe. Following combat, a soldier's perceptions may change—a majority of the world may now seem unsafe.'

"That's why returning vets may reflexively search alongside a US interstate highway for roadside bombs, only shop at Walmart at three in the morning, or worry to excess that their children's school will be attacked by terrorists. And it's why after hearing the stories of their patients, reliving the horrors of war, watching them endure pain and sometimes countless operations, medical practitioners can suffer from the same fears—whether it's the surgeon who heals the wounds, the psychiatrist who probes the mind for the source of anguish, or even the clean-up staff decontaminating and removing the blood from surgical tools. Combine that with homesickness, the high operational tempo of Landstuhl, the low tolerance for mistakes, the downtime when the mind takes over and remembers every awful experience. It's a dangerous, often unhealthy mix."

For many of the doctors and nurses I reached out to, even years later, they still haven't forgotten those who came to them broken and battered, some mortally wounded. Even though they did everything they could, they still feel they should have done more.

"Hardly a week goes by without my mind turning to one or another of the service members that I flew on medevac transport planes," wrote **Susan Fondy** ("'Two Someones?'"). "Names, faces, situations; they come back unbidden, sometimes during quiet times, other times during conversation; sometimes with sadness, other times with wondering, anger, frustration, or joy. This book is a tiny glimpse into the daily reality of the military medical professional and our service to our heroes, the front-line grunts."

The author Paul Gallico wrote in 1946, "It is only when you open your veins and bleed onto the page a little that you establish contact with your reader." For many who wrote stories for *The One*, the writing process proved to be just as painful, as if they were doing open-heart surgery with a rusty scalpel, as they recalled and related to their unforgettable patient.

"I do certainly have many stories (somewhat buried in the subconscious at this point) that are powerful landmarks of my medical practice," wrote **Anthony Pansoy** ("A Proud Father"). I spent a year in a very high intensity combat environment with much time 'outside the wire.'

"I felt as though my patient's story had to be told regardless of how angry and sad it would make me feel. I felt as though this might also help readers get a better understanding of compassion fatigue and how health care workers can become overwhelmed seeing traumatic combat injuries on a daily basis."

Dr. Yang Wang ("'Have You Ever Seen It This High'" and "'Cat Alpha—GSW to the Head'") wrote: "I felt it was impossible to sum up everything about my deployment in a single conversation when family or friends asked me, 'What was it like?' I needed a way to process through everything in some sort of methodical way, and putting discrete missions into written words was a way to try to sort all the random images and smells and sounds floating in my head into some semblance of a linear narrative. It was a start, but it was helpful, and so I'm writing more. I still get goose bumps when I think back on the things we saw and did, and I sometimes even tear-up with nostalgia for that punch-drunk mixture of exhaustion and excitement we carried stumbling off the plane at 0700, watching the sun rise over the Afghan mountains, after flying back-to-back missions since 1500 the day before and having crossed the entire country three times over. At this point in my life, I can't imagine anything in the civilian world that's going to measure up to all the ups and downs, frustrations and triumphs, losses and rewards that were all packed into those five months when I played my little part in the war in Afghanistan."

"Writing these stories reminded me of how privileged I feel to have been chosen to be a poly-trauma nurse," recalled Connie Bengston. "It has been a true honor to serve these men and women who sacrificed so much and worked so hard to fight back from debilitating injuries and make the best of what they have left. The easy part of writing these stories was recounting what I observed, what I was witness to, about the men and women to whom I was a nurse.

"The difficult part was going back in my emotions and thoughts to what it felt like for me to experience being a poly-trauma nurse. When I first sat with my laptop to recount that first story about the young Marine critically injured by an IED, I started to type just one word and immediately the tears flowed. I shut the computer off and returned to it later, but the subsequent tries weren't any easier. It was raw, it was visceral. I'd never before been asked to write something like this and it was foreign, and sometimes hard to comprehend! I had to figure out why it was so difficult. The conclusion I have reached so far is that I have given all I have emotionally and physically, and I'm fully invested in the outcome of those wounded warriors I would be assigned to care for."

Like many of the soldiers who volunteer for combat deployments, one doctor served multiple tours in several war zones, with barely enough time to get reacquainted with his family before it was time to head "downrange" again. In his emails he has hinted at so many stories, and maybe someday he'll retire and write his own book, but for now, he can't slow down, not even long enough to write just one of those unforgettable stories.

But for those who did take the time to write something for this book, an amazing thing happened, something that didn't necessarily come out in their stories, but which they revealed to me in correspondence afterward. Nearly all of them admitted that writing about the one patient they could never forget was emotionally painful, and yet it was also therapeutic, almost like a cleansing of their conscience, a clearing out of the cobwebs that had been tormenting them for all these years.

"While I often recount my war experiences, using them to train others to do the job I did, writing for *The One* opened many personal memories I had pushed to the side. Much of what I wrote came from my journal and it gave me the chance to read observations I haven't seen in years. Even better, I stumbled across an envelope containing all the letters and drawings my children sent that were hung on the wall of my tent. I was reminded how important my family is to me and the bond we have."

Dr. Stanley Chartoff During several email exchanges, Anthony Pansoy explained compassion fatigue to me. Others I've been communicating with mentioned burnout among health care providers, especially those who deal with trauma patients. While the intent of *The One* was merely to showcase the dedication of military medical personnel, this book also shines a spotlight on compassion fatigue.

For one doctor, he never admitted it to me, but I heard from his wife. Finally, she understood why he had built invisible walls so many years ago, and shut everyone out all this time, including her and their children. After writing his story, he decided maybe it was time to tear down those walls and reconnect with his family.

Again, my intention for *The One* was to pay tribute to those who care for our nation's wounded warriors. I should have been able to predict that many of the caregivers were emotionally wounded from dealing with so much trauma, and just maybe they too needed their own TLC: some more than others.

In one of my early deployments as an Army photojournalist, my immediate public affairs supervisor near the Korean DMZ was SFC Sheppard Kelly. Some days I dreaded briefing him on what I was working on or showing him what I'd written, because he never let me cut corners, never accepted anything but my very best. Looking back, more than anyone else, Kelly inspired me to love writing and respect everyone. He drilled into me that everyone is unique. Everyone has a story to tell. Getting them to tell their story is the real challenge.

Each story in this book is unique, and each author not only recalls a patient they could never forget, but they also reveal why. Some revealed more about themselves than they ever realized. Each of them and the thousands more who serve as military care providers work under extremely difficult situations for prolonged periods of time. On a daily basis, they rise "above and beyond" and face unimaginable challenges, both physical and emotional.

Army photojournalist Gary L. Bloomfield, on the Korean DMZ
PHOTO BY GALEN GEER

I can't help but think of a quote by Stephen Grellet (1773–1855), which may explain why these very exceptional individuals—those in military medicine—do what they do: "I expect to pass through this world but once. Any good, therefore, that I can do or any kindness I can show to any fellow creature, let me do it now. Let me not defer or neglect it for I shall not pass this way again."

One dictum I had learned on the battlefields of France in a far distant war: You cannot save the world, but you might save the man in front of you, if you work fast enough.

—Diana Gabaldon

The views expressed herein are those of the author(s) and do not reflect the official policy of the Department of Defense, or the US Government.